# PRAISE FOR
## *DESIRE: A MEMOIR*

'Jonathan Dollimore, a working class man who became one of our most thoughtful intellectuals, has written a memoir that meditates on sex, identity, boredom and ecstasy. It is a rich, sad, wise book.'

Edmund White, *author of Our Young Man*

'There is no resisting the pull of Dollimore's poignant memoir. He relates his compulsive experience of gay culture with raw candour and reflects on it with subtle refinement. This is a meditation about the desire for sex and oblivion and its complex relation to loss, depression, and suicide.'

Colin Thubron, *author of Night of Fire*

'A quietly startling memoir, though with no confrontational element. Jonathan Dollimore's scrupulous sifting of the past always tests ideas against experience, and finds more than once that disasters have a liberating effect. This isn't the sort of book you'd expect an academic to write, in fact it's almost the exact opposite of the sort of book you'd expect an academic to write, and much the better for it. I enjoyed it very much.'

Adam Mars-Jones, *author of Kid Gloves*

'At last it is here. We have waited too long for Jonathan Dollimore's sparkling, tender, deliciously funny and astute tales of the life of desire – in his own extraordinary journeys through time. All the mystery, miseries, and delights of lust and longing are exquisitely laid bare, in a memoir so riveting you will return to it again and again.'

Lynne Segal, *Birkbeck University of London, UK,*
*author of Making Trouble: Life and Politics*

'Jonathan Dollimore's story will touch, haunt and break your heart, though not necessarily in that order. And as if that were not enough, he tells it with such discipline, delicacy and directness that even as it becomes authoritatively his own, the story of his times starts to show through it, and then the story of mortal life and desire itself.... An awe-inspiring achievement.'

Ewan Fernie, *Shakespeare Institute, Stratford-upon-Avon, University of Birmingham, UK*

'There are many who will be fascinated to learn about the life of a brilliant teacher, writer, radical intellectual adventurer, who for many was a role model on how to think and do our work *differently*. Jonathan Dollimore made himself the inspiration for generations of scholars in multiple fields. This memoir is an incredibly powerful, open, self-aware, and beautiful piece of writing. More than anything, it is a gift of trust to his readers.'

Linda Charnes, *Indiana University, Bloomington, USA and author of* Notorious Identity: Materializing the Subject in Shakespeare

# Desire:
# A Memoir

## BEYOND CRITICISM

Taking advantage of new opportunities offered by digital technology and new insights from contemporary creative practice that take us from abstract theory back to literature itself, *Beyond Criticism* explores radical new forms that literary criticism might take in the twenty-first century.

http://thebee.buzz

Series Editors:
Katharine Craik (Oxford Brookes University, UK), Simon Palfrey (University of Oxford, UK), Joanna Picciotto (University of California, Berkeley, USA), John Schad (University of Lancaster, UK), Lilliana Loofbourow (University of California Berkeley, USA).

# Desire:
# A Memoir

*Jonathan Dollimore*

Bloomsbury Academic
An imprint of Bloomsbury Publishing Plc

# BLOOMSBURY

LONDON · OXFORD · NEW YORK · NEW DELHI · SYDNEY

**Bloomsbury Academic**

An imprint of Bloomsbury Publishing Plc

| 50 Bedford Square | 1385 Broadway |
| London | New York |
| WC1B 3DP | NY 10018 |
| UK | USA |

**www.bloomsbury.com**

**BLOOMSBURY and the Diana logo are trademarks of Bloomsbury Publishing Plc**

First published 2017

**British Library Cataloguing-in-Publication Data**

A catalogue record for this book is available from the British Library.

| ISBN: | HB: | 978-1-3500-2311-6 |
| | PB: | 978-1-3500-2310-9 |
| | ePDF: | 978-1-3500-2313-0 |
| | ePub: | 978-1-3500-2314-7 |

**Library of Congress Cataloging-in-Publication Data**

Names: Dollimore, Jonathan, author.
Title: Desire-a memoir / Jonathan Dollimore.
Description: London ; New York : Bloomsbury Academic, 2017. | Series: Beyond
criticism
Identifiers: LCCN 2016055227| ISBN 9781350023109 (pb) | ISBN 9781350023116
(hb) | ISBN 9781350023130 (ePDF) | ISBN 9781350023147 (eBook)
Subjects: LCSH: Dollimore, Jonathan. | Critics--Great Britain--Biography. |
Intellectuals--Great Britain--Biography. | Philosophers--Great
Britain--Biography. | English teachers--Great Britain--Biography.
Classification: LCC PR55.D65 A3 2017 | DDC 306.092 [B]--dc23 LC record available at
https://lccn.loc.gov/2016055227

Series: Beyond Criticism

Cover design: Alice Marwick

Typeset by Fakenham Prepress Solutions, Fakenham, Norfolk NR21 8NN

To find out more about our authors and books visit www.bloomsbury.com. Here you
will find extracts, author interviews, details of forthcoming events and the option to
sign up for our newsletters.

A starlit or a moonlit dome disdains
All that man is,
All mere complexities,
The fury and the mire of human veins.

– W. B. Yeats

… in my arms till break of day
Let the living creature lie,
Mortal, guilty, but to me
The entirely beautiful.

– W. H. Auden

Every damn thing you do in this life, you have to pay for.

– Edith Piaf's last words

*For Marek*

# CONTENTS

# PREFACE

I first came across the work of Jonathan Dollimore sometime in the middle 1980s, as a student *fresh* – if that is the word – from Tasmanian adolescence. The book was *Radical Tragedy*. I recall well its abrasive strangeness. It struck me as a stern, arresting, upbraiding missive from a more grown-up world, one where people who had survived things told their truth, with a keen eye for reigning lies, familiar somehow with the facts of metal and rust.

I liked the mood of its intelligence, often peremptory and impatient, keen to strike at the ore, and for all its formidable grasp of Theory – as I had only just learned to call it – just a little bit savage. Here there was nothing airless, nothing airy either. You could somehow hear the chains jangling, the cables that move the machine, the *work* active and unfinished in the work. I was a young man, barely a man, and I had never come across anything quite like it.

If I had to choose a word to describe how this writing felt to me at the time, the word I would choose is 'masculine'. Back then I would have meant by this something vague and probably reactionary (in part, reacting against the abstraction of academic thinking). But it has proved apt in much more embracing ways. I know of no contemporary writer who has probed so fearlessly the experience of masculinity – what it might, must, could, should, would, shall entail – whatever the imaginable scope of this experience, and whatever the suppressions or permissions or sublimations. Such is the burden of Dollimore's trailblazing trilogy, *Sexual Dissidence* (1991), *Death, Desire and Loss in Western Culture* (1999) and *Sex, Literature and Censorship* (2001). His supreme subject has become the modalities of male desire.

He was always much more than a literary critic. His first fame was from his work on early modern drama, often in fruitful collaboration with Alan Sinfield. But I always suspected that plays *per se* weren't quite the thing that grabbed him. The plays seemed a symptom, even a ricochet, of things much more urgent. Dollimore had done things, or was doing things, and his writings exploded out of the experience, just as the writings he was exploring had done in their own way. He was far ahead of the game.

It strikes me that a single question, or perhaps a single experience, is turning at the heart of much that Dollimore has written. The experience is desire, and its consummate action is sex. What would it be, what would it take, to construct an ethics, to make or to unmake a life, to write even a sentence faithful to the implications of that experience? Faithful to its furious confusion of cherishing and carelessness, dominance and submission, imitation and audacity, structure and chaos, creation and waste, action and its lapsing, fulfilment and annihilation, interpellation and individuality, ideality and flesh? Imagine a body of work as the detonation of sex, at once an opening to another's power and a discharge that takes no prisoners. Imagine taking on the difficulty of such metaphors, their violence and complicities, such that they are more than metaphor, such that they compose the world we must encounter. Something like this, I think, has been Dollimore's quest.

And now comes *Desire: A Memoir*. In truth, it should come as no surprise that Dollimore would write such a book – so confidential and unguarded, so tender to the undead past – but still it is surprising. In it there is no mention of Dollimore's other writing, and barely of his *career* in the *academy* (two things he holds in the deepest suspicion as refuges of disintegrity and compromise). Instead, Dollimore seeks to touch the desire that has fed him and led him in his journeys. It is less a conventional autobiography than a refraction of the lived life's collisions and entanglements, with the recollecting mind a kind of diving bell, risking the pressure of memory.

Some of these journeys have the glamour of scandal and transgression; others are unapologetically humdrum, working in a Dunstable factory, tinkering with an engine, the sedulous discoveries of the untutored mind (it is, among many other pleasures, a moving reminder of how the most probing modern sensibilities are often autodidact and suburban). Many episodes combine the mundane and dangerous with devastating effect, as something routinely decried as obscene or criminal is experienced, in the season of its occurrence, as the simplest daily pleasure or exaction. One thing is always true: Dollimore does not measure experience by the precepts of others. These precepts may encourage him – a constitutional rebel – to enter a supposedly forbidden space. But once he has entered, he is always there alone, even in company, feeling out the membranes of the new.

In the past, Dollimore has written of his boredom with theories of the body – so bodiless – and his impatience for modes of thinking more sensitive to what he has called the body's 'recalcitrance'. There is much of such recalcitrance here, of the unyielding facticity of body. We find him surviving a heady night, waking amid detritus, escaping detection and moving on to the next encounter, inexplicably entire. But along with this, necessarily, comes the body's vulnerability, the knowledge that life is a mortgage. Death here is never an abstraction.

Dollimore's desire is motivated backward and forward, a phenomenon (or perhaps phenomena) of loss as much as possession, of the casting mind as much as the questing body. Memory itself can become the lodestone of desire – not always equally, for some memories are more casually or equably borne. But there are episodes here of the deepest passion – passion meaning suffering – such as when the last image of a beloved young man is seared like a brand upon his mind, unrepealable. Tenderness is the watchword, the tenderness of flesh and the tenderness of attentive consciousness, both in and beyond the moment. At times Dollimore's memories evoke the same wistful mood as Faustus when, gazing upon a virtual Helen, he sees the 'topless towers' that can finish only in extinction or sees a face that launched a thousand ships, every last one a desire in commission. Indeed, Dollimore's 'desire' frequently reminds me of Plotinus' dizzying version of the fall, when souls revolted from the One in an act of self-originating audacity, hungry for metabolism, inventing time (a factitious illusion) and spawning the yearning fragmented individual soul, wracked by matter, condemned to a body, reaching for the One from which they recoiled.

*Desire* is also, explicitly and immanently, an engagement with depression, as a kind of corollary or anticipation of the final self-loss. Suicide is attempted, remembered, feared, desired, revoked, retried. It is chastening to read of Dollimore's recurring despair in the years 1990 and 1991, when he tried to kill himself a number of times, with varying degrees of intent. These were also the years when he wrote and published his masterpiece, *Sexual Dissidence*. In this context, it is humbling to return to his wrestle in that book with Augustine, and, in particular, Augustine's theory of privation: the idea that sin has no substance; that to err from God is a living annihilation; that to experience perversity is to move as the dead. Augustine famously stole pears for the hell of it, but found a second life in God. But then what happens to the rest of us, who cannot, who do not wish to, escape from the waylays of desire? In writing as he does Dollimore is, I think, literally, fighting for his life.

Among many other things, here is the 'beyond' of criticism – the passions that inspire it, the engagements it sublimates, analyses, at times disguises, and, of course, some things that exceed its idiom entirely. Quotations from favourite poets – Yeats, Stevens, Herbert, Shelley – rise from the fabric of the prose, strangely radiant, as though with the dew still upon them. *Desire: A Memoir* should send readers back to Dollimore's earlier books – each, likewise, fresh as dew and often as salty as the fluids we render for our loves. But it also stands alone, not finally assimilable to any critical discourse. In this it takes its place in a counter-tradition of dissident, transgressive (often homosexual) autobiographical portrait, such as those of flawed heroes like Wilde, Gide and Genet. And so it is perhaps fitting that, far better than anything I could say, a passage from Genet's *Prisoner of Love,* quoted at the close of *Sexual Dissidence,* beautifully suggests the longing in Dollimore's new and brave work:

*What sort of beauty is it these lads from the shanty town possess? When they're still children a mother or a whore gives them a piece of broken mirror in which they trap a ray of the sun and reflect it into one of the palace windows. And by that open window, in the mirror, they discover bit by bit their faces and bodies.*

– SIMON PALFREY
NOVEMBER 2016

# ACKNOWLEDGEMENTS

My greatest debt is to Ewan Fernie, without whose thoughtful correspondence during some bad years I'd never have written this memoir and might have ceased writing altogether. Along the lines of the dubious saying that he who saves a life becomes responsible for it, variously attributed to ancient China and Hollywood, I find myself cheerfully, if somewhat ungraciously, laying at his door my book's shortcomings as well. I'm also grateful to Rachel Bowlby, Linda Charnes, Adam Mars-Jones, Bharat Ravikumar, Lynne Segal, Jill Sharp, Colin Thubron, Edmund White and Gregory Woods for reading and commenting on the ms, and offer belated thanks to James Brown and Patricia Sant for putting up with me, in Sydney, those years ago. Earlier drafts of parts of some chapters appeared in *Sunday Telegraph*, *London Review of Books* and *Massachusetts Review*.

# 1

# Life-changing accident

I had gone looking for my mother and found her outside, sitting with Tony in the family car. As I approached, unbeknown to them, I saw that Tony was trying to have sex with her. One of several complications swirling from this scenario was that at the time, Tony, an adult friend of my parents, was also having sex with me.

Having just read that, the reader won't be surprised to learn that the desire of my title involves sex. However, this book is also about other things, other desires, including the ambition of a barely literate boy, who'd left school at fifteen to work in a factory, to escape that destiny and become a writer. What I hadn't realized until I came to write about this ambition, was the extent to which it, too, had an erotic component, inspired as it was, at least in part, by my relationship with Tony, between the age of fourteen and fifteen. Tony was an interesting man, ex-RAF, nomadic, far more knowledgeable than any other adult I'd encountered, including all of my school teachers, and also seemingly genuinely interested in teaching me things – as well as having sex with me. It was under his influence that I started to read thoughtfully for the first time. He introduced me to writers like Kipling, Somerset Maugham, Graham Greene, Thomas Hardy and T. S. Eliot.

The cultural influence that Tony exerted on me would now be construed as 'grooming'; and maybe it was, but it was also what made me want to learn to write. I did experience it as a desire, perhaps because it was so closely related to my sexual encounters with him, which weren't demanding or complicated, and mainly consisted in him sympathetically helping me to orgasm. I liked that well enough to sometimes lie awake at night when he was staying with us, hoping he might come to my room to do it again. What led me to put a stop to it was coming across him and my mother that day in the car, with him trying to make out with her. I watched them for a few moments before quietly retracing my steps. It was clear that my mother was resisting, and in a resigned and firm kind of way, which gave the strong impression that it wasn't the first time she'd had to do so. I was impressed by this and after a little thought simply decided to follow her example. That was it: no more sex with Tony. On the face of it then a triumph for matriarchy, with Freud and trauma nowhere in sight. I didn't feel personally betrayed by Tony's attempted seduction of my mother; nor have I ever felt damaged by the sex he and I had together. Of course, I realized that, at the very least, he was betraying my parents's trust in having sex with me, but, at the same time, that, too, was attractive to this adolescent.

It was early spring when I saw Tony and my mother in the car and there's an adjacent memory, unconnected at the time, yet merging with it in hindsight: it was either on that same day or one near it that I noticed for the first time, or properly, the scent of daffodils, exquisitely perfect but elusively faint, leaving me wanting more. And yet, when I went back to them, there was no more, and soon they were faded and the scent gone completely. Wanting the more that wasn't there: desire can be like that – and this is a book about desire, always more than sex even, or especially when experienced or expressed sexually.

A few years later, I came across a letter from Tony to my parents. It was left lying about, but still I shouldn't have read it. He was then living abroad and was ill, dying actually, and the letter was a bitter one. He'd previously written to ask if he could come and stay with us – he wanted to return to England, perhaps to die there – and my parents had refused.

This letter was an angry repudiation of my father and included the disclosure that, although he'd never mentioned it before, he'd always known my father had had an affair with Tony's ex-wife, when they were all young newlyweds and living together just before the war. I don't know for sure if this was true, but knowing my father it probably was, and if so, Tony's attempted seduction of my mother, and his successful seduction of me, might have been an act of revenge on my father. If so, it was one that maybe succeeded indirectly and unwittingly, because Tony did hasten my growing apart from my parents. This wasn't directly sexually related, and had more to do with something else he'd given me, a record of Stravinsky's *The Rite of Spring*. My parents didn't listen much to music, but insofar as they did, liked soothing, popular classical tunes, wincing and blanching at anything discordant, strident or even just loud. Although my own musical interests were a bit wider, I still heard music through their ears, especially if they were in the vicinity, and often even if they weren't, and I did so in an intuitive anticipation of, or wanting to preempt, their discomfort.

When I first played *The Rite of Spring*, I did a double wince, one for my parents, one for me, it sounding pretty strident to my ears as well. Something though kept drawing me back to it and then suddenly I got it – not gradually but instantly, now hearing it completely differently, as if with someone else's ears, someone radically different from my parents and from me, too. The discordant became dynamic, vital, exhilarating, exciting, maybe dangerous, too, especially as the sacrificial story which (I later learned) the dance expressed. That led me to become fascinated with Nijinsky who choreographed the first performance. I was hooked. It wasn't so much that 'I' had at last heard it correctly, but rather that hearing it differently had somehow made *me* different. I'd heard it exhilaratingly as someone else; it had changed me into that someone else. I'm sure Tony had no idea of what he'd initiated, and I never told him because by this time he'd gone abroad again. However if his sexual interest in my mother and myself was indeed revenge against my father, then, in giving me that record, he'd kind of succeeded, more so than through his sexual interest: symbolically, and even actually, it was the single most significant factor in my separation from my background. In a sense, I left home the moment I heard, in vibrant dissonance, an intimation in that music of being alive differently, of art as an articulation of libidinal energies which brought them to consciousness differently, perhaps to consciousness for the first time. Later, with a more 'trained' ear, I'd hear the repressive energies of that music, but not then. Thereafter, for better or worse, reading, writing and music retained some tenuous link with desire, and even danger, if only to the extent that I later found myself drawn to those who wrote most compellingly about desire and danger. Tony may have been corrupt and corrupting, but I regret nothing about my relationship with him.

But there was something else that happened a few months later, also crucial in my setting out to write – a motorcycle accident which could have killed me, yet paradoxically both saved my life and profoundly changed it.

I remember coming round, lying on the road, the bike on top of me, the sound of car doors slamming, running feet, more than one person leaning over me, telling me to lie still. I insisted I was OK, kept insisting, and despite their efforts to stop me moving, somehow got to my feet, staggering in the direction of home. At that point, there was more numbness than pain, but my left leg wouldn't work properly. The accident had happened only a few hundred yards from home on a stretch of road I'd travelled, by foot, on a cycle and in the family car hundreds of times.

I'd just turned sixteen a few weeks earlier and that particular day was an August bank holiday and I'd been working at home with a friend, Terry, on our motorbikes. It was a beautiful day and for a long while afterwards, I could never trust such days; irrational though I knew it to be, even then, I resented that chasm between the day's beauty and my pain. I needed some spare parts for my bike and borrowed

Terry's Triumph to go the mile into town to get them. It was on the way back that it happened, although to this day I still don't know exactly what did happen. I remember riding the bike up to about 100 yards before the point of the accident, but from then until I regained consciousness afterwards, it's a complete blank, total amnesia, and a mystery, too, since no other traffic was apparently involved and it was a straight road (generally speaking, boys fall off motorcycles on corners or when they hit things). Unfortunately for me, I'd not been thrown clear of the bike but become entangled with it as it slid along the tarmac. Wearing only a t-shirt and jeans, with no helmet, I was badly hurt. On my arms and legs and forehead, the skin had entirely gone and my shoulder was gouged to the bone. There were long gouges on the tarmac too, where the bike had dug in, and they remained there for years, until the road was resurfaced. By a weird coincidence – the kind that ultimately irritates because it teases with a significance you know it can't deliver – one of the motorists who had come upon the scene of the accident, worked at the motorbike shop I had just visited, although he was off work that day. He knew me but hadn't recognized me at the accident because there was so much blood on my face.

As I staggered home, my left leg gave way altogether and I think someone caught me before I fell, breaking the fall. I saw my mother running towards me; Terry, waiting for my return, had heard his bike approaching and had heard, but not seen, the accident. There was wetness in my eyes which prevented me from seeing my mother properly. I may have been crying, but as I wiped away what I thought were tears I realized it was blood, or rather assumed it was because I could taste it. (As children we were taught to suck a bleeding wound to cleanse it, so I knew well the taste of blood.) That look of terror on my mother's face as she helped me home – did I see it or imagine it? Or half see it and half imagine it? She got my clothes off, or what shreds were left of them, and, because there was gravel in the wounds, was just about to help me into a bath when the ambulance arrived. She mentioned later that she burned the clothes.

As I write this I've just realized, with the son's remorse, but also the writer's fascination, that there would be two further occasions when my mother would be called upon to dispose of my bloodstained clothes. The second time was a car accident just a couple of years later; the third was after a suicide attempt. The grief I caused her on that last occasion was the greatest of all, and one about which I feel only remorse. In later years, I sometimes fantasized about being able to die with my mother; as a kind of reparation – not just for the hurt I had caused her, but also for what life had done to her. Many years later, she went swimming with me in New Zealand. I went into the sea first; turning around to look for her, I shuddered to see her looking so frail and old in the cold water. It was love that I felt, but the shudder was for her and for my own mortality. Part of what bonds the boy to the mother is his narcissism, something she nurtures, consciously or otherwise, and sometimes, the stronger the bond, the greater his narcissistic wounds later on. I was wounded then by her frailty being also my own mortality because it was something she couldn't protect me from, nor I her.

The ambulance arrived and I heard a medic shouting to my mother something about the bath – not a good idea. By then though, I was naked and he took some woollen blankets from the ambulance and wrapped me in them. The next memory is waiting, seemingly forever, in Accident and Emergency at Luton and Dunstable hospital, with my father nearby trying to comfort my mother. Being a holiday, there had been more accidents than usual, but also less staff to deal with them. That was how things were then and we – my family – would have been the last people to question such arrangements. By the time I was seen by a doctor, the blood had congealed and the woollen blankets were stuck to the wounds. As a nurse tried to remove them, I screamed in pain and begged her to put me to sleep, by which I meant I wanted an anaesthetic though unable to think of the word. She must have thought I was asking for a mercy killing because she loudly reprimanded me for even thinking such a thing and then muttered more quietly something about her not being a vet. But I did get an injection of something and thankfully lost consciousness.

The wounds from that accident were bad enough for the doctor to ask my father to break it to me that I was going to be badly scarred for the rest of my life. He did so, and at the time I thought this might enhance my otherwise lowly status in the world in which I moved. Actually, though I still have scars to this day, I healed amazingly well. When I returned to the hospital as an out-patient the same doctor said my skin had remarkable healing powers. I was proud of this, too, being at the time hungry for any kind of distinction. For the same reason, I was disappointed that the scars I was left with weren't more attractive. The one over my right eye made the lid droop slightly. To be attractive, scars have to be of the right kind in the right place and mine were neither. Incidentally, many years later, a surgeon who had x-rayed my left knee in preparation for an operation asked me when I'd fractured it. I told him I hadn't, he gently begged to differ, and it dawned on me that it must have happened in this accident, but gone unnoticed. As I said, it was an accident which could have killed me but which both saved and changed my life, and in ways I'll come to later. First a few general words about this memoir.

*Desire: A Memoir* comprises episodes of a life, significant experiences of things in tension with each other, if not in outright opposition, and all in the orbit of desire. It includes the squalid and the precious, the suicidal and the elated, the sublime and the absurd, the tender and the callous and the dangerous and the beautiful – the last two being, perhaps, the most important of all, if only because I encountered them in even closer proximity than the others. It's not a complete or even a coherent life story: I suspect that the more coherent a memoir becomes, the more tailored the memories. I've never had the discipline to keep a diary, but occasionally, if an experience was intense enough, I'd write it down at the time. For years, this would have been on scraps of paper – whatever was nearest to hand – and lots of them have been lost or discarded over time. Some of the ones that have survived comprise part of this story and are distinguished from the rest of the narrative as indented text in the present tense.

The accident when I was sixteen saved my life because, although as soon as I was fit enough, I rode motorcycles again, and that included riding some very fast machines very recklessly, it was never again with that same sublimely ignorant adolescent abandon with which I'd ridden legally in those few days before the accident, and illegally at night, from the age of about fourteen onwards. That previous abandon was in part due to a lucky escape I'd had riding an off-road bike on the fields adjacent to where we lived. Me and my brothers would buy up worn out but still powerful motor-bikes for just a few pounds and then race each other around a roughed-out track on the field. The bike I had, a 1950s' Aerial 500 single, had long before lost its brakes and the secret, if you wanted to slow down, was to scrub off speed by laying the bike low and sliding into and around corners. One day, I went into a fast corner too fast and simply couldn't scrub off enough speed, careering off the track and into a very thick and high hedge. The bike and I climbed up the hedge, snapping branches as we went. I eventually came to a stop about 10 feet off the ground, pinioned in place by numerous broken and jagged-ended branches, any of which could have pierced me. I waited there, expecting any second to feel pain and see blood, but neither came. Miraculously, every single spear-like branch had missed me, and the only hurt I suffered was in climbing down. I left the bike where it was and gradually the hedge grew around and through it, and it disappeared from sight, though not before my father saw it and threatened to ban me from riding. The exhilaration of having escaped scot-free was intense and encouraged a recklessness in me which, with hindsight, could only end badly. My relationship to motorbikes at the time was so passionate as to be an *amour fou*. Crazy adolescent desire – what Jack Kerouac memorably called 'the long wavering spermy disorderliness of the boy' – led me to become fixated with riding them, or at least sitting on them, holding them between my legs. When I first rode a bike, around the age of fourteen, I concluded there was nothing else in the world I wanted to do. When I got off it, I craved to get back on, and could think of little else until I did. This is what I'd been missing, what could and would answer the inarticulate yearning. It was desire as madness, and I say that because I can remember the passion, while no longer being able to retrieve the experience. No matter how reckless, if you can still retrieve the experience of past desire, then it wasn't madness. I now can't – and it was. Yet to this day, I understand entirely Toad's serial infatuations in *The Wind in the Willows*.

Unlike that field escapade, the road accident left me with a nascent sense of how to survive the desire to experience danger, of the skills necessary to do so. In later life, one negotiates dangerous situations mainly by avoiding them. When young – assuming you're given the time, and I nearly wasn't – you quickly learn the skills that give you a fighting chance of surviving the dangers you actively court. That's the essential thrill of embracing danger: surviving it while getting as close as possible to it. It's psychobabble to assume those who flirt with death have a death wish. Some might; others definitely don't. The scene in *Rebel without a Cause*, where they drive cars to a cliff edge, bailing out at the last possible minute, is exactly right. In later years, teaching young people, I often wondered at what really makes that difference between the young as innately reckless as distinct from innately cautious. In the world I came from it was, to some extent, a class difference. But later on I re-encountered another kind of recklessness in the sexual promiscuity of the gay night life in the early years of HIV/AIDS, and that had little to do with class differences.

My proudest possession was a BSA Gold Star 500cc single, in racing trim. It was bought from a man in Luton who had dreams of going racing, but never did. Or rather he went once and frightened himself so much he was incapable of trying again. The bike had languished in his backyard until I heard about it and persuaded him to sell it to me. It was fast for the day, being capable of around 70mph in first gear alone, and with questionably handling on the limit: for an inexperienced sixteen-year-old, it was lethal.

Speed is addictive in a quite precise sense of the word: it compels both repetition and escalation. To get the same high as previously one always needs to go that bit faster. More exactly, one always needs to go that bit faster because the *real* high, like so many of the objects of desire, is always tantalizingly just out of reach. Back then our life chances, and, even more important to us at the time, our chances of avoiding serious injury, depended in part on how skilled we were in pursuing this always elusive high. But only in part: the lorry that pulled out in front of one friend on the A5 was unavoidable, no matter how skilled he was, and had he not been doing the best part of 95mph he might have avoided it. Speed kills, and it maims. To us, disfiguring or disabling injury of a severe kind was more feared than death itself. It's often said, in this regard, that the young believe they are immortal. For us it was more mundane than that: we were so immersed in our lives, we didn't give death – as distinct from injury – much thought. But then we didn't give much thought to anything outside of our passions; for as long as they gripped us, we lived in the present in a way which was as spontaneous as it was ignorant.

At weekends, we'd ride into London, to a club there run by the famous 'Ton-up Vicar', as the tabloid newspapers called him. One visit was doubly memorable: the vicar himself got up on a chair, calling the bikers to attention. Apparently someone had actually part-sawn through the frame of another's bike in the expectation that it would completely fracture at speed. The vicar told us, in a sad and downcast sort of way, that this was a bad thing to do. At the time, I was sitting at a table with an obese and highly perfumed man who I knew even then to be gay. He mentioned that I should come to one of the vicar's special away-weekends. I felt no distaste and much curiosity, something which has impelled many of the significant experiences of my life. Sadly, the invite was interrupted by the vicar's address and never firmed up. From there, my biker friends and I would occasionally go to Soho, where we would watch the prostitutes in diffident awe. We'd neither the money nor the courage to do anything more than watch. At the time I was still a virgin, or at least I think I was, not being entirely sure even now of what comprises a boy's virginity and what determines its loss outside of the conventional scenario of having intercourse with a woman. If that scenario is indeed the determining one, it has the intriguing consequence of making me still a virgin, notwithstanding the sex I'd had with the boy next door and Tony.

The accident changed my life because while I was recovering in hospital, I decided to leave my job in a car factory and become the writer I'd recently decided I wanted to be, under Tony's influence. I now realize it was the morphine and probably other pain killers that were responsible for this. The nurses were free with them. There I was, in much pain, immobile, covered with ugly wounds, warned I'd be badly scarred for life, yet with these intense feelings of euphoria and even a kind of omnipotence. For the first time in my life, anything seemed possible. I hated the factory where I was working and realized that it was possible for me to leave it. Yes, I would leave and become a writer! The situationist cry from the streets in 1968: 'Be realistic – demand the impossible!' was still a few years off, and anyway I didn't encounter it until years after that, but it seems to encapsulate what I felt in that hospital bed. There were lows, too, in the hospital, however, especially when I was moved to a ward entirely given over to others who had also been injured in motorcycle accidents. I remember weeping uncontrollably for reasons I just couldn't explain and my euphoria would quickly turn into a wrenching frustration at not being able to help those who had been more severely injured than me. This was before the time of compulsory wearing of crash helmets, as we called them then. And although we sometimes wore protective leathers, that was more of a sign of allegiance to 'rocker' culture than reasons of safety. Jim, the boy in the next bed to me had been in plaster for many months. In an accident, which hadn't been his fault, he'd been hit sideways by a car; his girlfriend had been riding pillion and the bike ended up crushed up against another vehicle. Both Jim's legs were badly smashed and his girlfriend was also injured, and was somewhere else in the hospital. When relatives came to visit him, they spoke encouragingly of her recovery, but even I could detect that this was mainly for his benefit.

At the time of the accident, Jim was building a bike to go racing. This was of great interest to me because my brother, Richard, was doing the same. So Jim and I wiled away a lot of time talking about the spec. of his bike and his aspirations for it on the track. On the face of it, the accident hadn't deterred him at all; but I found I was behaving a little like those relatives, encouraging him in a way which was less than completely honest, so I suppose I detected something forced in his optimism, as well as theirs. Then one day, he complained of new pains in one of his legs. When the doctor came and sniffed it, presumably for gangrene, Jim started to cry with such utter anguish that he was quickly moved elsewhere. I think both he and I had smelt it, too. I never was able to find out what happened to him.

If the experience of pain, injury and the stench of mortality was one consequence of the desire for risk on the road, it never cancelled its erotic charge. Maybe that's not the best way of putting it; I mean that, as an adolescent, these risks made me feel more alive, more connected with others and in an immediate physical way. Sensuality might be a better word. Years later, in Italy I witnessed a near accident. Two boys on a powerful bike – both without helmets and in t-shirts only, just like me when I had my accident – were speeding on a main road when a car pulled out in front of them: the rider swerved with lightning, unflustered reactions, laying the bike so low that I thought he must surely drop it. But he didn't, and this was partly because his pillion was in a perfect physical sympathy and balance with him, and so effortlessly, that in the middle of the manoeuvre, the pillion gave the driver of the car a languid one finger insult as they missed his front bumper by an inch or two. So yes, 'erotic charge' maybe too strong because it involved an eroticism which was in a way as disinterested as aesthetic attraction is sometimes said to be by philosophers: there was no desire to 'have' or 'possess' these two boys or to connect with them in any way; it was just an intense, detached appreciation of something sensuously beautiful. But yes, still erotic in a way because that sensual sympathy or synchrony of rider and pillion was, for me, always erotic.

In an obvious sense, the sudden feelings of unlimited potential I experienced in that hospital bed was a drug-induced illusion. And yet I did leave the factory, and I did, eventually, become a writer, although the euphoria of the hospital morphine only carried me through the first stage: leaving.

## '... their best/Desires'

I had left school earlier, at fifteen, in the Easter of that year, to take up an apprenticeship at AC Delco, a nearby subsidiary of Vauxhall Motors at Luton. A so-called 'careers advisor' had visited school and asked what I was interested in. Cars and motorbikes, I replied with alacrity. And without further ado, he gave me an application form for an apprenticeship at Vauxhall Motors, which I filled in and duly sent off. By the time I was summoned for interview, my passions had broadened to include fishing, and the evening before the interview I'd been taking part in a schools' competition on the Grand Union Canal. I had caught a decent-sized fish but had no net to keep it in. My friend offered to take it to the judges there and then and I agreed. (I still experience that excitement which wants an achievement publicized now, immediately). On the way, he decided to hold it under the water every so often, so that it didn't die before the judges saw it, and, of course, it escaped. By the next day, I still hadn't got over the disappointment. Quite how or why the several elderly men who interviewed me allowed me to get onto this topic I don't know, but it took up most of the interview, and I must have told my story of the fish that got away plausibly enough because they offered me an apprenticeship. I felt great pride – apprenticeships were at the pinnacle of aspiration for secondary modern schoolboys, and I was the only one from my school who got into this particular factory. But we had no idea of what was coming: the decline of the British motor industry, and British industry generally, and the eventual full closure of the Vauxhall car plant in Luton in 2000. The factory where I worked was demolished in 2005 and replaced with a housing estate.

The reality of factory life was a debilitating shock. I had never been as miserable as when I started there. Work began at 7.30 a.m. which meant I had to get out of bed at 5 a.m., cycle a mile, and then get a bus which took me to work. I left my push bike at the back of a local shop. I was mostly located at the Dunstable factory, but was also taken over to the Luton one, which was much larger. Most mornings, I so didn't want to go that I'd have to roll out of bed onto the floor when the alarm went off: only the shock of doing that would awake me from a sleep both depressed and regressive. Being in that factory was like being caged. It was noisy, hot and vast, so vast I initially got lost when sent on errands and was reprimanded for skiving off. I still have dreams of being lost and anxiously trying to get back to my work station. In these dreams, time is short; in reality, it went agonizingly slowly. I'd play tricks with myself to try and make it pass more quickly. It would be exaggerating to describe that factory as Dickensian, and yet it was closer to the factories of his time than to the high-tech ones of today. There's a passage in *Hard Times* which I first read with groaning recognition:

There was a stifling smell of hot oil everywhere. The steam engines shone with it, the dresses of the Hands were soiled with it, the mills ... oozed and trickled it ... And their inhabitants, wasting with heat, toiled languidly.

How I recall the machine oil – its smell, stain and slipperiness attached to everything; the way it enervated, as did the heat from the machinery, heat which the oil seemed to permeate and make heavier; as did the heat of the sun that oppressed the fiercer for shining through skylights stained yellow by oil. Oil reduces friction, but in that factory it made everything harder and in the most tactile of ways.

For me, the only thing that came close to relieving the tedium was the humour of some of my workmates, those who were older and who'd been there longer. Some of them were superb mimics – they actually honed their skills while working, gradually perfecting the voices and mannerisms of television celebrities and factory management. What made the mimicry so endearing was an extra streak of parody; an exaggeration with no intention to deceive, only to capture, to disclose a truth beneath the surface, behind the physical presence. So, for instance, there was a celebrity whose public image was one of apparent modesty. Their mimicry of him exaggerated the modesty in a way which revealed him as actually boastful, and in ways which today, on social media, are common and commonly mocked as humblebrag, but which then were less obvious. It was mimicry as an art form.

At the secondary modern school I went to, we were told that we were practical kids who would keep the country going and become the backbone of the future – in contrast to our grammar school counterparts who were brainy but useless pen-pushers. We willingly embraced that rationalization of the school system and our disadvantaged position within it. But we were rightly proud of our practical skills and, to this day, I feel mild contempt for those who make a virtue of being hopelessly impractical (working in universities, I have met quite a few). But because apprentices in that factory were employed mainly as cheap labour, we were actually taught few skills there. What skills we did learn, we got outside the factory, from the evening and weekend culture of the motorbike and car. We bought secondhand and we stripped and rebuilt; that's what I was doing when I had the accident. The practical skills of the mechanic and the engineer were real, and we respected and wanted them; whereas work in the factory was repetitive and boring, so much so that this other culture of the bike and the car was a compensation for it. But it was also an extension of it. In other words, it was an escape from the very industry of which it was also a consequence; real human skills and values grew from oppressive social realities, compensating for them, but also reinforcing them. It would be pretentious and plain wrong to say we exemplified the affirmative aspects of Marx's famous dictum that people make history, but not in conditions of their own choosing. But we did exemplify its less optimistic implications – the idea that those unchosen conditions not only remain embedded in our very efforts to escape of them, but also determine the form those efforts take and the skills which result. Thom Gunn once wrote a poem which, in its wonderful testimony to those skills, is to my knowledge unique in literature. Called 'All Do Not All Things Well', it describes two 'auto freaks' from the American underclass who dismantle cars on driveways. Neighbours disapprove of the mess and get them evicted. Gunn regrets their going:

-Certainly not ambitious,
Perhaps not intelligent
Unless about a car,
Their work one thing they knew
They could for certain do
With a disinterest
And passionate expertise
To which they gave their best
Desires and energies.
Such oily handed zest
By-passed the self like love.
I thought they were good
For any neighbourhood.

Those lines are a beautifully perfect description of the culture. It's been in backyards, on driveways and the street itself (neighbours permitting) that this culture flourished, and not in the factory, where the soul-destroying drudgery of assembly line work was the fate of most. In later life, I have reconnected with the kinds of people Gunn describes and some of them I respect as much and sometimes more than the few academics I've admired. Never was the two cultures stand-off more apparent than here. In Gunn's poem, a new neighbour (an outsider) wants them evicted because of their detrimental effect on property prices. She might well have been an academic: in more than thirty years in the humanities side of universities, the attitude towards those skills which I encountered was mainly one of ignorant, patronizing condescension. Just occasionally a student from the science side would dismantle a car in a campus car park only to be moved on by the authorities, as were Gunn's auto freaks. Among the younger academics, disdain for this culture verged on contempt because of its supposedly obsolete 'masculinist' values. Those same academics were also the ones quick to brand any intense friendship between the men of this 'masculinist' culture as repressed homosexuality. In truth, sometimes it might have been, and yet sometimes it almost certainly wasn't: some of the most loyal and selfless friendships I've ever known were between working-class young men who, insofar as anyone can ever be sure of these things, really were straight.

That morning at home, working on our bikes just before the accident: I remember other such mornings especially Sundays, when myself and my three brothers would be working on whatever it was we currently had – my eldest brother Patrick by then with a car, Richard with his racing motorbike, Robert working on one of his guns. Through amazing determination and effrontery, Robert got into an apprenticeship with what was then one of the finest gunmakers in the world – Purdey's in London. He was, and is, an immensely gifted craftsman. We worked on and with machinery, seeking that 'passionate expertise' to which we gave our 'best/Desires and energies'.

Outside of this passionate expertise, I was sadly wanting: gullible, ignorant, bigoted and naive. Still, looking back, I respect that passion: desire as work or, in the philosopher's more exalted term, praxis.

# Leaving

After the accident, there was huge pressure for me to graduate to a car. For my mother, the great advantage of us boys' so graduating was that it significantly increased our chances of staying alive and/or unmaimed. (I don't think my father gave it much thought.) For me, however, it was the opportunity to at last participate in a popular local game of knocking over bollards on the nearby M1 motorway. This was the opposite of skittles or bowling; the idea wasn't to knock them all over, which was anyway too easy (you just ploughed into them); no, the challenge was to take out just one at a time, and that got more demanding the faster you went. Predictably then, the first major car accident wasn't long in coming. I called home from a phone box late at night, just after it happened. I could hear the trepidation in my mother's voice as she answered. I think she had sensed – had certainly feared – the accident even before I'd phoned. I remember her telling me after we'd all left home that she used to count us in at night, not coming through the door, but listening in the stillness of the night for the approach of our bikes or cars.

My car at the time was an old Austin Healey sports car, and driving it on unfamiliar road on a wet November night, I'd hit some wet mud dropped on a corner by tractors exiting from an adjacent field gate. As I skidded off the road, I could see, with some relief, that I was going through a pretty thin hedge into a field beyond. Could be a lot worse, I thought – a fraction of a second before hitting a small tree I'd failed to see in the centre of the hedge. It was only about 9-inches thick but that was enough because my front wheel had hit it side on, on full lock, at its base. I went up and through the windscreen, losing consciousness for a while, getting badly cut and bruised, but with nothing obviously broken. Some local farmers, the same ones who had dumped the mud on the road, eventually appeared and pulled the car out of the hedge and fork-lifted it to their yard. When I finally got around to recovering it, I found that someone had stripped it of valuable parts, probably the same farmers. Despite that, and the fact that it was a write-off, and that I had only third-party insurance, like Gunn's auto freaks I rebuilt it on the drive outside my parents' house. It took a long time.

In the factory, I was based in the apprentice workshop. We were overseen by a man in his early sixties. I recall most clearly his hair: a short, back and sides cut, combined with advanced baldness meant there wasn't actually much of it. What remained was combed across the scalp and glued down immovably with Brylcreem. The first task he set for every apprentice was to file a hexagonal bar down into a square. When you thought it was square, you took it to him and he decided if it was square enough. If it wasn't, he'd send you back to keep filing. His reasons for sending you back were only loosely connected with the accuracy of your filing. If he thought you might be a troublesome type, he'd repeatedly send you back to file some more, even after you'd got it square, which meant, more often than not, that you'd subsequently file it out of square – which was further reason to send you back. In that first exercise were encapsulated the rules of factory life, and to some extent the rules of 1960's industrial Britain.

When on returning to work after the accident, and still somewhat emboldened with my morphine-induced vision of other possibilities, I told this supervisor that I wanted to leave, he didn't take me seriously; in fact he said 'fuck off'. I had to tell him a second, then a third time before he would listen. He thought for a while and then, remembering my accident, asked: 'Did you hit your head in that bike smash you had?'

'Yes', I replied.

He gestured for me to follow him to his office. With a rare expression of concern, in complete earnest, and with all his customary ignorant authority, he advised me: 'That blow to the head has unhinged you. You need to see a psychologist.'

To be fair to him, he was half-right, except that it wasn't the concussion so much as the morphine which had 'unhinged' me; drugs had allowed me to think the unthinkable. It was a heady moment when, with the aid of drugs, pain dissolved into possibility, and without them I'm sure I wouldn't be writing this. When I finally bade the supervisor farewell, his last words were that I was doing a stupid thing that I'd always regret. I half-believed him and certainly didn't walk out of those factory gates with confidence, the morphine confidence by now having all but deserted me; the possibilities it had opened up remained, but it was hard to keep faith with them. After all, my desire to be a writer was based on little more than adolescent ignorance and sensitivity: things affected me fairly intensely and I had this underlying sadness, and I believed these two things made me somehow unique. Of course, they didn't. Moreover, my writing skills were non-existent. Most secondary moderns were bad schools, and mine had been one of the worst. But it wasn't all the school's fault; at home and in my background, there was just no culture of learning anything that wasn't of a practical nature. Whatever the reasons, however, the truth was that I was barely literate and my writing aspirations were unrealistic to say the least. But then many of our desires and ambitions are delusional to a greater or lesser degree, and if the delusion and our failure to see it for what is can eventually thwart us, they also help us persevere. Were I to encounter my sixteen-year-old self now, I'd fall in love with him for those very reasons and (chastely) seek to mentor him.

I saw that supervisor once again, and once only. It was about two years later, after I had lucked into a job as a trainee newspaper reporter. I had just had my first byline, when the reporter's name is attached to the story. Passing through Dunstable on a job, I dropped in and proudly, nervously, showed it to him. He looked at it for a while and then called all the apprentices in to show it to them, saying, 'Look at this! I always knew this lad was capable of better things. Not like you shower.'

He carried on in this vein for a few moments before dismissing them. I don't recall before or since feeling such an agony of embarrassment: my proud achievement had been turned by the supervisor into a betrayal of my former workmates and a humiliation of both them and me. I can't entirely condemn him: when I later found myself in largely middle-class and academic circles, I encountered the more sophisticated (and successful) likes of him many times over – people whose instinct was to keep others down but who were more than willing to identify with, exploit and even take credit for, their success, if and when it came. And, if anything, the hypocrisy of these people was the greater because poisoned by a knowingness, envy and advantage which that factory supervisor didn't have.

Of those other apprentices, there's one I remember especially. Steve was older than me and kind in that gruffly reticent way which was the only way kindness could be shown there. A few years later, we re-encountered each other, both clinging precariously to, and several metres up, an advertising hoarding at the Silverstone motor racing circuit (for a better view). We only mutely acknowledged each other. I regret that. Some say they regret nothing about the past, this lack of regret being a corollary of living life to the full. I've never understood or trusted the claim. If living fully is more than just appetite, it involves empathy, as well as passion, which, in turn, drive, even as they are in tension with, each other. The instance of this untaken opportunity to reconnect, to say thank you, is only a small case in point, but realizing it now prompts in me an awareness of how this life-story is sometimes pressured by regret shading into hurt, both about things I could and should have done differently, and things over which I had no control at all. To regret nothing is a form of disavowal, albeit an empowering one if it can be sustained. Regret can be as powerful and inevitable as longing itself; it may even be indistinguishable from a form of regressive longing. It's been said that nostalgia is death. Regret and remorse are also kinds of death, or at least link us to it. Maybe a radical forgetting of the past is the only way we can be fully alive in the present. If we are lucky, we sometimes live like that, completely lost in the present. But I know of no sensitive person who has ever sustained that kind of aliveness across a life, or even a significant part of it.

# 2

# Loss and change

The feelings of loss started at an early age. As a child, I don't think I could articulate them at all, never mind exactly; probably the best I could do, if asked, was to admit to feeling sad, while being unable to say why or about what. Later, I became aware of it as a sense of loss somehow always in excess of anything in particular. Older still, I was able to articulate it a little more clearly, but this wasn't only a question of better understanding: the feeling itself had become more acute, more intimately and threateningly connected with desire, along with depression: a feeling of something lost that, paradoxically, had never been consciously possessed or even known. Going in search of it was like moving towards an ever receding horizon. It was a feeling of permanent incompleteness, of happiness as permanently elusive: *then* it was experienced as inconsequential, *now* as irrevocably gone; always in a past where it never quite existed as such at the time. That's when I thought about it or tried to articulate it; at other times I felt it as an underlying boredom, a curiosity about things other people thought were best left alone, and an attraction to risk. But it was such thoughts which, perhaps more than anything else, made me want to write. The few thoughtful friends I had at the time thought I was just screwed up – and they weren't wrong.

The house where I grew up was midway between the small village of Billington and the town of Leighton Buzzard, in

Bedfordshire. Originally the land on which the house had been built had been a pit from which clay was excavated, and later, in the First World War, a barracks was built there for soldiers. A one-storey make-shift building made entirely of wood with a felt-tarred roof, it was really just a large shed, and was set in about an acre of ground, deliberately left quite wild to encourage wildlife, which opened onto surrounding countryside; it was rural, though not especially idyllic. Nearby were some small lakes, sand pits and a narrow gauge railway and engineering workings which supplied the legendary sand of that area. About 100 yards along the road from the house was a crossing for a railway line. It was close to this crossing that my motorcycle accident happened. So we lived on a kind of border, what is now sometimes called edgeland: on one side of the railway line was open countryside for as far as the eye could see and as far any youngster could roam; on the other were the sand pits, engineering works and, beyond them, the town. We trespassed in the railway and engineering works when they were deserted, sometimes risking life and limb in the process. On occasion, we'd be playing on the railway track, sense a tremor in the rails and look up to see a steam train thundering down on us. My family finally left that house in 1977, when my parents emigrated to New Zealand where my two elder brothers were already living.

About a decade after we left, I was travelling on the M1 with my partner, Alan, and I suggested we make a detour and go look at the old house. Quite why I thought to do this is surprising; at the time my life was in one of those 'don't look back' phases, when the intensity of the present led to a temporary forgetting of, or indifference to, the past. But go we did and, by a remarkable coincidence, we arrived on the very day that the house was being bulldozed to the ground. Flimsily built, it didn't take long. Shortly after that the surrounding area was flattened and concreted over to become a huge parking lot for intercontinental lorries. Now nothing recognizable remains of our life there except the odd tree that we climbed. The fields that we roamed have also disappeared, either under new housing estates or turned into massive pits from which the sand has been excavated, some of them thousands of yards across, looking like massive water-filled bomb craters.

Since that day of returning to see the old home being demolished, I've dreamt about it time and time again. Ordinary rather than disturbed dreams, they are, none the less, a kind of mourning. I have revisited the place again since, walking around, trying to remember what used to be where, which was impossible to do, so savaged was the landscape. Once though, I thought I recognized, alongside a housing estate being constructed, a small patch of ground bordered by a hedge where as children we had once built a secret hideaway. Before I had time to confirm if it was indeed the place, a security guard manhandled me off the site. Not for the first time, I realized the futility of return – the place was there, but there was nothing to be gained from it apart from a visceral experience of change and loss. For me, it's always been a mistake to return to a place of significance. Whatever draws one back is irrevocably gone, and all that's there is a blank, indifferent absence. Knowing this, I'm still drawn back.

Obviously the loss experienced in relation to my home went much deeper than the specific place. Thoughtful people sometimes endeavour to search for themselves, saying, for instance, 'I want to find myself, to find out who I really am.' I've never felt inclined to do, or say, that. If I experience myself at all, it's as something contingent and provisional, held together precariously by a shifting, conflicted consciousness, which doesn't feel all that interesting in, and of, itself. More exactly, for me the individual life, including my own, is of interest mainly to the extent that it resonates with life in the larger senses of the word, the life which passes through it. That's also true of the life of desire. When I started reading philosophy and literature, I soon realized that whatever we're thinking and desiring as individuals has been thought and desired before. So, if along the way, I cite philosophers and artists, this isn't to dignify my narrative with learning, but because they came

before and have put it better than I can. I soon found loss
to be one of the pervasive themes of our culture and immor-
talized in some of its greatest myths. We must love in order
to live but, at least for the irreligious, to love is to love what
inevitably vanishes, turns to dust. If religion claims to redeem
the loss while at the same time giving us the greatest mythical
expressions of it, that's surely because it's from the experience
of loss religion partly grew. Adam and Eve are expelled from
Eden with the consequence, it's said, that we humans forever
feel its loss. But the myth that most appealed to me was that
told by Aristophanes in Plato's *Symposium*: his central idea is
that originally we were whole, but subsequently and traumati-
cally cut into two. Aristophanes is speaking specifically of 'the
lover of boys', but adds that his account is applicable to all
those lovers whose 'soul ... has some other longing which it
cannot express, but can only surmise and obscurely hint at'.
Originally, he says, there were three sexes: male, female and
hermaphrodite. They were formidable and hubristic creatures
who even dared to attack the gods. To weaken them, Zeus cut
each of them in two: 'Man's original body having been thus
cut in two, each half yearned for the half from which it had
been severed.' It is from this distant epoch, then, than human
love, as we know it, derives – 'the love which restores us to
our ancient state by attempting to weld two beings into one
and to heal the wounds which humanity suffered'.

As with most myths, there were aspect of this one which to
the uneducated younger me seemed strange and inexplicable,
but what I took from it was the idea that desire, originating in
a division, a wound, a kind of death, becomes an experience
of present/projected lack rooted in present/remembered loss.
Caught up somewhere between past loss and future lack,
desire remains unsatisfiable and comes to consciousness as the
seemingly inescapable condition of restlessness and dislocation.
It's as if desire is subjected to a pull in opposite directions,
forwards to find what one is lacking and backwards towards
the original state of wholeness. It seemed to me a beautiful
expression of the sense that desire, even consciousness itself,

is predicated on a lack, an absence, a baseline of permanent dissatisfaction, verging on pain, cancelled only in death. More mundanely it suggested why, when we try to seize the day, it slips between our fingers, like grasping at the wind, the intense present being always desired, yet strangely elusive. It's tempting in memory to misrepresent the past as more present than it was, whereas, in truth, we are looking back to a time when we were looking forward. The past never quite existed as memory – memory as consolation – would have us believe.

Family history may well have played a part in both my life-long experience of depression and that pervading sense of loss. I was the youngest of six children: two girls and four boys. The girls were the first and third children and both died in early infancy. I'm still not sure how or why. Though not exactly a secret, my mother barely spoke of them, that being her way of handling grief. It's a painful irony of the family that children experience its losses even, or especially, when under-standing little about them; with the best of intentions, the child is protected by the parents from a grief which, despite or because of that protection, they internalize. Shortly before she died, my mother did tell me about a day when she was walking the several miles to the girls' graves with my eldest brother, Patrick. This was shortly after the second daughter had died and she was crying and he asked her why. She never told me what, if anything, she said in reply, only that, from that day on, she decided never to visit the graves again; she would, henceforth, devote herself to her living children. As I grew up, I became aware of the grief she must have felt. But it was so long ago; the grief was past. Except it wasn't. For some reason, the graves of the girls were unmarked. Perhaps my parents couldn't afford gravestones, or maybe they were removed. In the late 1990s, Patrick researched local records and found the original graves and my sister-in-law, Jennifer, arranged to have a headstone erected there. When I first visited those graves, I wept uncontrollably and completely inarticulately.

Young creatures, new forms of life, die in infancy all the time in their millions, billions: in the futile attempt to make this brute fact of endless death signify, one ups the figures until they cease to signify and is then tempted to rationalize the fact by acknowledging that the death of new life is the most natural thing in the world, not least in the sustaining of other life. Death obliterates life, but so does life itself, and not only in the food chain. Then again, a thousand seeds fly in the wind, some fall on stony ground and never germinate, while those that fall on fertile ground grow and die in a full life cycle. Yet others still fall on sparse soil – the cracks between the pavement – beginning to grow, only to then die prematurely from lack of nourishment. That, too, is natural. Yet *one* sentient creature will grieve so deeply for the loss of *one other*, especially one who dies prematurely, as to threaten its own survival: Heathcliff literally tearing at Cathy's grave; Hamlet mourning his father and being told that his grief is unnatural in its excessiveness and realizing that it's our very unnaturalness which makes us human.

When my mother was old and living on the other side of the world, in New Zealand, I would awake in the night with a sudden sense of her grief all those years before when she lost those two children. Impossibly, I wanted to make reparation, redeem her from that loss, stop her from ailing, from dying. There may have been another reason for this grief, however. My being born at all was, in a way, a consequence of their deaths. Had they lived, I doubt my mother would have wanted a sixth child, nor perhaps even a fifth or a fourth. After my father died, we found a letter he had kept from my mother, written just after their second daughter had died. It was 1945, and he was still abroad, serving with the RAF. Because of wartime disruption in communications, he received the letter telling him his daughter had died before the earlier one telling him she had been born. In that second letter, my mother talks of the struggle to overcome her grief and her conviction that she will one day have a daughter who lives. So probably her last three children, all boys, were attempts to have another girl. I was the last. I was very close to my mother – perhaps too close. I always felt her love for me and my brothers to be unconditional, so much so that it never occurred to me that she must have been initially disappointed that I wasn't a girl. Actually that's not quite true: when I was old enough to think about these things I realized I was, to some extent, a surrogate daughter for her, that being one reason we were so close. That made me rather proud, and my only concern was that I was as good a surrogate as a boy could be. And if anyone reading this concludes that here is the cause of my homosexuality, my honest response would be that I have no idea if they are right, and I am happy if they are. In fact, if one's sexuality needs a cause, I can't think of one I'd prefer.

The deaths of those two daughters was repressed in our family, partly I think because they happened during the war, which also was repressed, my parents never speaking of it. That wasn't unusual of course, but in this case may have had an unusual cause: as I grew up I heard rumours that my father, who was a military policeman, was so hated that there was even plot by other servicemen to kill or at least harm him. These were rumours only and I don't know what, if any, substance there was in them. Because of my parents reticence about the war it seemed to me, as a child, an age ago, a different age – the equivalent of another century. I knew, of course, that my parents had experienced it, but I was convinced they had done so as different people, living in a different age. In fact, the war ended only three years before I was born. As I've grown older and the war has become further away from me in actual time, in significant time, it has come ever closer. The older I get, the more I think about it, the death mutilation and misery it caused and the unmarked heroism of the many who endured it. Sometimes this is so intense it's as if something repressed is coming back into consciousness. It's like trying to redeem a sin of forgetting and I experience an almost desperate wish to remember, which then becomes resignedly defeatist as I realize that the war is just one such episode in human history and that it's impossible to truly remember them all; that numerous such episodes have already been forgotten or translated into 'heritage' history. It's like a camera suddenly panning back from something specific to a vista in which all specifics merge into the distance and then disappear, to be replaced with a generic sign. Likewise, we glimpse the poignancy of grief and loss which wounded millions of lives for their duration, but is now becoming a fading memory within the greater culture, like an anonymous photograph of someone loved, which has yellowed and faded on the mantlepiece, and is now lying on the floor of a junk shop where its recently deceased owner's possessions have been offloaded by the callous relative doing the house clearance.

There's a still further possible reason for this sense of loss, although here I'm conscious of possibly myth making. My birth was traumatic, not to say lucky, and I was probably originally one of two. I knew about this from an early age, but it was only shortly before my mother died in 2008 that I found out what had happened. This is what she wrote:

> I was well into pregnancy when late one evening I had labour pains and a lot of bleeding. The doctor came and confirmed I had miscarried and actually gave me an injection which he said was to make sure it was complete. A couple of months later I had not had a proper period and found I was putting on weight. I saw the doctor and he told me I was about four and a half months pregnant, and the 'miss' I had had was almost certainly a twin. He had only heard of one other case in his medical career. I had been very depressed after the 'miss' and was delighted to find there was still a baby who was born at full term though small at 5 lbs.

That was me.

# Journalism

After leaving the factory, I bummed around for a while and started to read – novels mainly, including those of Graham Greene and Somerset Maugham, but also some poetry, including that of T. S. Eliot. I went to these writers for no other reason than that Tony had introduced me to them only to find that they used so many words the meanings of which I didn't know. So, with a rare impulse of self-discipline, I started to write down every word I didn't understand, after first looking it up in the dictionary. The sheets of paper were soon piled high. Looking back over them, I'd find I'd written the same word down several times, obviously forgetting its meaning after looking it up. But slowly my literacy improved.

At the same time, I'd gone into the offices of the newspaper in my home town several times and asked for an interview with the editor. I was emboldened to do this by the example of Robert, my brother who, despite all the odds, and through audacious pestering, had managed to land an apprenticeship at Purdey, the London gunsmiths. Eventually the editor granted me an interview. It was in the early afternoon and he was already drunk. He didn't say much, except that I was a tall boy for my age, which was an odd thing to say because I wasn't. I wondered if he was hallucinating as well as drunk. I said I wanted to be a newspaper reporter and asked what were the chances. He said there weren't many openings but he'd bear me in mind. Some months later I was living rough in Bournemouth with two other friends and about to hitch hike to France with one, having read somewhere that Paris was a place where you went if you wanted to be a writer. I rang home to tell my mother of these plans and not to expect to see me for a while; she told me that the editor had called the day before and wanted me to start work the following Monday. I later learned that one of his reporters had left abruptly and I was the first person he'd thought of. This was an incredible piece of luck. If he'd advertised the job every other candidate would have been better qualified than me: I really was barely literate. I'd failed the 11-plus and the 13 plus, and all the other exams I'd taken at school (with the exception of religious knowledge and technical drawing – both of which were given out for free in those days) and really couldn't

write. Anyway, I went home, got my hair cut and my
mother bought me a suit, shirt and tie.

The first few weeks there were agonizing. The editor
quickly realized that he'd made a mistake in hiring me, but
he also knew my father via one of the town's pubs, and felt
he had to give me a chance. There were two reporters there,
Ann and Dennis, who helped cover for my total incompetence
and, to this day, I owe them both. The reporters would put
their copy in a box on the editor's desk, in a separate office;
he'd then sub it and send it off for a combination of manual
and mechanical typesetting in the same building (I'd joined
another industry heading for extinction). After depositing
my copy, I would sit at my desk trembling inwardly, and
quite probably outwardly, too, waiting for him to shout for
me to come to his office, whereupon he'd reprimand me for
the numerous errors I'd made. He shouted at me a lot, but
I struggled on fearfully, eventually learning to put sentences
together and to spell passably well.

My education began when I got that job as a newspaper
reporter. It was hugely instructive in (some of) the ways of the
world and it helped me grow up. Along with my other limitations, I was naïve about pretty much everything. It wasn't
that I'd had a protected upbringing; as I have mentioned
elsewhere, as children we were allowed to run free and it's
remarkable that we survived as unscathed as we did. But it
was an *isolated* upbringing, growing up in the country, and I
only really moved between there and school. As a young child,
I was also chronically shy. To my terror, I was pressured into
minor roles in two school events: in the first, I was required
to parrot half-a-dozen words and I simply couldn't speak
them, my mouth drying and throat physically constricting;
in the second, I pissed my pants and, thereafter, was left
alone. Although later in life, I developed reasonably effective
masks, I never did rid myself of that early childhood fear of
public speaking, although thankfully I did learn to control
my bladder. I disliked school, but was reasonably obedient
there, at least until my last year. Recently, looking at some old

school reports, I found that they were about as bad as they could get: 'Tries hard. 4/10' was a typical grading. 'Delinquent and lazy' would have been preferable to that.

As a reporter, however, I got to see how a small town worked – how its establishment was made up of class, respectability, prestige and money; its petty corruption, mutual backscratching and so on. It was a revelation. I saw potentially embarrassing stories about eminent local people mysteriously kept out of the paper; I had policemen ask me not to report compromising accusations against them in court, with offered favours in return. I'm now ashamed to admit that I was fairly compliant in the system I was getting to know. Actually that's not quite true – I would willingly bend the rules if I liked someone, but not if I didn't. On one occasion, I refused a policeman's request to keep an embarrassing story about him out of the paper – because I didn't like him and I knew he was corrupt – and in revenge, he roughed me up one night when I was leaving a party, grabbing me and slamming me up against a nearby wall, literally lifting me off the ground in the process, as tough guys typically did in films, squeezing my throat so I couldn't breathe. I never considered reporting him because he would only have denied it or have said that he was only restraining me because I was drunk (which I was) and more importantly, I'd have been cold-shouldered by the rest of the force. We needed them as much as they needed us.

Many if not most other public figures in the town were like our editor in deferring to those with the most money, prestige and power – because life was easier that way. They opted for a reasonably quiet life. I could understand that and had no wish to make their lives even more difficult than they already were. But there were others, like that policemen who roughed me up, along with certain council officials, directors of powerful local businesses, to name but a few, who were corrupt in the sense of persistently breaking the rules, often to the extent of hurting others, in pursuit of their own self-interests. There was also the ubiquitous practice of the cover-up – not the audacious conspiracy, just lazy complicity with the status quo of provincial life. Here's an example ...

There was a man in the town, Edward, who was openly gay, or at least openly camp (remember this was at a time when homosexuality had only recently been decriminalized). Everyone knew he was 'queer', and most enjoyed his company: he was flamboyant and entertaining. When I was younger my father, who wasn't averse to having a drink with this man himself in the pub, had warned me to keep away from him. It was also the time when every self-respecting straight man 'knew', in virtue of his own masculinity, that every queer man was also a child molester. Obviously, that piqued my interest and, thereafter, whenever I saw Edward in town, I'd greet him with a smile, and once a smile plus a tentative wink, but it never worked: he'd respond with expressions ranging from the bemused to the alarmed and hurry on.

One morning, Edward was found drowned in the local river. An inquest found that late the previous night, he'd left a local pub, adjacent to the river, and fallen in, probably because he was drunk. Behind the scenes, it was acknowledged that there was evidence suggesting he'd been pushed or thrown in after some kind of liaison with someone in the pub car park or along the river bank. Possibly, because the identity of that person was known, but more likely because it was not and no one was inclined to mount the necessary investigation to discover it, a verdict of accidental death was thought preferable all round. When I later pressed a policeman on this, off the record, he just shrugged and said that sooner or later that kind of person was bound to come to no good.

Occasionally life as a reporter was exciting, though, and very occasionally even slightly risky – if, for example, people didn't want to talk to us and we were too persistent, they might throw a punch. Undoubtedly though, the greatest risk to my life and limb came from the editor himself for reasons I'll explain shortly. He wasn't actually an aggressive man; he rarely bit, but he barked a lot and was at his worst on Monday mornings, when we were all under pressure, putting the paper to bed (it appeared weekly, on Tuesdays). He'd always come into work in a foul mood and those three or so hours were tough on all of us, but especially me. On Mondays, but also other days, too, we'd all relax around midday when he left the office to go across the road to the Conservative Club; we could always tell when he was heading there because of a genuine lightness in his step as he passed through our office to the door. It was unmistakable: when he walked, usually he leaned slightly forward, at least when sober; with this lightness of step, his posture would tilt even more so, as if he were about to pitch forwards. He'd come back at any hour in the afternoon, always half-cut; sometimes he'd not reappear at all that day. If he did, we could always judge how drunk he was by how upright his posture was. He must have been around the age of sixty, and had never learned to drive up until then. Unfortunately, he decided to learn not long after I joined the paper and because by then I had a full licence, I was roped into accompanying him while he practiced his driving skills around town. This was where danger to life and limb came into play. He was, without doubt, the worst driver I have ever sat next to. To begin with, he had no mechanical sympathy, revving the engine to ruin in second gear, for example, rather than changing up, and this on a completely deserted straight road. More worryingly, he was oblivious of the most basic rules of road craft, crossing red lights and stopping at green; careering across junctions over which he had no right of way; going around gentle corners as a snail's pace and, in turn, blasting around sharp ones on the opposite side of the road, sometimes driving up onto the pavement. He braked furiously when there was no need to ('just to be on the safe side') and didn't brake at all when there was desperate need to ('don't want to hold things up'). He'd back into hedges and walls and sometimes other vehicles, *and just not notice*. I was never allowed to criticize and only permitted to advise if he was in a good mood. It wasn't that he was a belligerent or aggressive driver; he was just radically, totally, incompetent. Add alcohol and he was lethal. Once he backed into a ditch and sat there for a while, foot to the floor, engine screaming, rear wheels spinning futilely, the car pointing significantly upwards from the horizontal. I knew better than to say anything, and anyway I was speechless from suppressed mirth. Eventually, he turned to me and asked what was wrong. I told him gently that 'we' had reversed into a ditch. He thought for a long moment, looked at me again, and with an expression more of perplexity than irritation, asked, 'Why?'

For the most part, however, life as a reporter in that provincial town during the 1960s was interesting rather than exciting and it could be said that, like many others who lived through those years, the 1960s largely passed us by. I did discover Bob Dylan, although my passion for him was solitary. Only fairly late did I discover another fan, another junior reporter on a paper in the next town. But he was alarmingly beautiful and aloof with it, and I never really had the confidence to talk to him about Dylan. Probably just as well because I could empty a busy pub once I'd got started on the singer's lyrics. A recollection: sitting up all night in another friend's flat drinking and listening to Dylan's *Blonde on Blonde*. The window of the flat, on a first floor, was adjacent to a street lamp and the forlorn, slightly flickering orange light it shed through the window at night is now, for me, inseparably associated with life back then in that town.

There were interesting interludes. One of the more memorable was also the most embarrassing. Early one afternoon, I'd gone to an imposing detached house to try and interview a business man mired in a controversy over a local development scheme which had gone wrong. We weren't sure there was a story in it, at least not one we could print. The man wasn't at home, but an attractive woman was. I assumed at the time it was his wife, but that may have been wrong. Whoever she was, when she realized I was after a story that would almost certainly prove compromising, she did the opposite of what most people do (shut the door) and asked me in, showed a flattering interest in me, became solicitous of my wellbeing and, within a short time, had completely disarmed me. I remember trying to convey to her what was so great about Dylan's lyrics (wince) and before I knew it we were making out on her sofa. She was much more experienced than me, of course, and also the other women I'd been with, both of whom had been my age or younger: the several hours that I spent with her were bliss. It was an unexpected encounter for an eighteen-year-old boy, in a provincial town, in 1967. However, after a few hours, she sent me packing with no story and not a chance in hell after that of getting one. Back at the office, it was tricky explaining why I'd been gone so long with nothing to show for it, especially since I wasn't good at deception. She, on the other hand, had staged managed the whole thing and I'd been completely taken in – *even* to the point of believing she was interested in Dylan's lyrics, or rather me expounding *on* Dylan's lyrics and *that* was more than embarrassing, it was mortifying, infinitely more so than being professionally compromised. And yet, it had also been exciting. I loved the unexpectedness of it: the surprise sexual encounter blatantly at odds with its context; the way it relieved, surprisingly and wonderfully, the tedium of the every day. So I felt elation, too, felt that bit more alive as a result. Later, I'd find a similar kind of elation in gay cruising. More than once when finding myself in an unanticipated embrace with a man, I'd remember that woman, and with gratitude.

In general, the work I hated most was sports reporting. It was the convention that a reporter would actually attend the matches of the town's football team, both home and away. So on Saturday afternoons throughout the winter, I'd have to stand around various pitches across the area, along with a gaggle of loyal supporters, watching the game. I blame those afternoons for retarding my homosexuality by years, quite possibly as much as a decade: I could only see those male footballers as ugly, macho and graceless. There was never an attractive one among them, at least not to my eyes. I've never really got over how utterly unappealing they were and I seem to be the only person who doesn't find footballers attractive. Back then it was something to do with the way their competitiveness always seems to be on the edge of a hysterical, petty belligerence – that, and the terrible shorts they wore. In isolation, a young man's knees aren't his most attractive feature, but passable in the context of the whole; on their own, and badly set off by those shorts, they are simply off-putting. The ballet-style tights worn by American footballers are a huge improvement and I've never understood why they can't be adopted by Europeans.

Anyhow, this complete alienation from the game meant my attention would frequently lapse and, if the grounds were blessed with a pavilion (or hut), I'd spend time there gloomily stitching together the clichés of the football report quite independently of the game unfolding, far too slowly, outside. That meant that occasionally, after a game had finished, I'd find myself unsure of the final score, and rather more often, of who had actually scored the goals. We had to give a running account of the match in the report, and I doubt I would have survived getting the score wrong because I'd have had to manufacture the game which produced it. As it happens I did manufacture the game report anyway – that's what I'd be doing in the pavilion or hut – but so long as it was flattering enough to 'our' team and the basics, including the final score, were right, no one minded. So, on the Sunday (the copy had to be in first thing Monday morning), I'd telephone the team manager and pretend to enthuse about the game. From the ensuing discussion, and prompts from me like 'did you think the final score was fair?', 'who do you reckon scored the finest goal?' or 'what did you say to the team at half time?' and 'how did individual team members feel about their game?', I'd piece together the match, the scorers, and the final score. I was, in fact, becoming cynical.

Cynicism was endemic in the journalists I knew. Some people in that town were cynical because they were intelligent enough to know what was going on, while being powerless to do anything about it. The journalists I worked with were rather different – their cynicism was a rationalization of their circumstances and was self-empowering, meaning that no scruples were ever allowed to stand in the way of a good story. This was most apparent with those who worked for the national papers. I got to know some of these during the biggest story we ever covered, the so-called 'Great Train Robbery' of 1963. It took place just outside our town. A gang of fifteen robbers stopped a Royal Mail train and stole from it more than £2.5 million (equivalent to nearly £50 million today). At the time of the robbery itself I was only fifteen, but I was working on the paper when some of the robbers were caught and committed for trial at the local magistrates' court. The London newspaper journalists came down to cover the story and relied on us for local information and for phone lines to London. They were stereotypical: hard-bitten, hard-drinking and deeply cynical. Before that, I'd nurtured thoughts of heading to London and trying to get work on a national paper myself, but not after getting to know them. They sneered at every idealistic aspiration that came their way, and did so through reference to the stuff of their trade – 'the real world'. They were, in their own eyes, and above everything else, hardcore realists, but in my eyes they were defeatists and failures, not least because they had zero interest in things like Dylan's lyrics. I knew, of course, that there were also some very different kind of journalists in London, working for the so-called 'quality press', ones with integrity and determination to tell truth to power, but they were way out of my league.

Working on that local newspaper was, as I've said, an incomparable education and helped me become half-literate. But after about four years, I knew I had to move on. Now, at last, I was ready for the other kind of education, the kind I'd failed at school. Throughout those four years, I'd continued to read and now I wanted to commit to that – to study, to read writers and philosophers who grappled with the Big Stuff. And, hopefully, to become a different kind of writer myself. So, just at the moment when promotion was in prospect, along with a decent income, I decided once again I had to leave, although now there was no morphine impetus, just the realization that to stay would be to get locked into small-town life for good, and, just as importantly, that I didn't want to become a hardcore, cynical realist. I was idealistic in a way, an adolescent and narcissistic kind of way. But I was also once again bored, restless and now with aspirations to answer with learning that underlying sense of something missing, something lost. I wanted something else. In fact, I *desired* something else: it really was that libidinal. If it hadn't been, I'd never have had the courage to leave. I didn't consider university; no one in my family had ever gone and at that stage it just wasn't a viable option. So I signed up to a GCE A level course at what was then Luton College of Technology. It was a difficult decision, and not made easier by the fact that on the day I signed up for the course, and had to explain to the first tutor I met what I'd been doing previously, he assumed the only reason I was there was because I'd been sacked. In his eyes, and those of others, including my father's, mine was an inexplicable backwards step. While there, I realized that some of the other students on the course were taking it in order to qualify for university, so I decided I'd do that, too.

# University

Only one university, Keele, offered me an interview. (Sussex, the university which some years later, gave me a job, rejected me not once but twice, when I tried to get there as a student. I mention this by way of encouragement to anyone else trying to get somewhere from the outside.) I had decided to study English with Philosophy. I had a vague but confident belief that philosophy would help answer some of the Big Stuff questions that I'd been ineffectually addressing to myself. With an interview pending, I clearly needed to find out what philosophy at university entailed. So the day before the interview, I went to Luton public library to find out. Among the handful of titles, I found one book with dust jacket blurb that went something like this:

Some people think philosophy is going to answer their questions about the meaning of life. This is a mistake. What philosophy can do however is to help you decide whether such questions are themselves meaningful. Quite often they are not.

For someone who had chosen philosophy as a subject precisely because I did expect it to answer questions about the meaning of life, I found this discouraging. I took the book on the train to Keele but never read it. I remember reading Herman Hesse's *Steppenwolf* instead. I was interviewed late in the day by a woman from the English department and a man from Philosophy. The man had a pipe. Both looked bored. The man's first question, I now know, is the one you ask when you can't think of anything else to say or haven't yet read, or can't recall, the student's application form: 'So why do you want to read philosophy?' Suddenly I so wished I'd read that library book, but all I had to go on was the blurb.

'Well' I said gropingly, 'Some people expect it to answer their questions about the meaning of life'.

'And what about you – what do you expect?' he replied suspiciously.

'Me? I … I don't expect it to answer questions about the meaning of life.'

He began to pay attention. Emboldened by my own duplicity I pressed on: 'Actually,' I said, 'I would hope it might help me to decide whether any of those questions people ask about the meaning of life, are themselves meaningful questions.'

'Interesting,' he said.

Warming to my topic, I took a risk and went just a tad beyond the authority of the book blurb. 'In fact,' I said, 'I shouldn't be at all surprised to find out that some of those questions are pretty silly.'

'Excellent!' he cried, and with that wandered off to get some tobacco for his pipe.

That just left the woman from English. She asked me what I thought of *Othello*, the Shakespeare text I was studying. If I'd spoken the truth I would have told her about how this was my first ever encounter with Shakespeare; that I had bought a copy of the play in a Luton bookshop and sat in a car park in the October gloom, anxiously seeing if I could even understand the language let alone the play; that I was relieved to find I could understand it, just about, in a halting kind of way; that, even so, the play seemed frustratingly absurd. And then, I should have told her about how I discovered three months into the course that my girlfriend was having an affair with another boy, which threw me into such a fit of sexual jealousy that I made a very nearly successful suicide attempt, and about how when I was allowed out of hospital and back to college, the theme of sexual jealousy had become so painfully relevant that *Othello* made too much sense to me – so much so that I could no longer even read it. Obviously, I said nothing of all this – only a very shrewd operator could successfully feed something so humiliating into a formal interview. Anyway hadn't I learned, on the hoof, and only moments earlier, the value of duplicity in this interview? So, instead, I showed I knew a bit about critics A. C. Bradley and F. R. Leavis (siding judiciously with the latter, like you did in those days). I was in.

Both English and Philosophy at Keele were uninspiring. I'm speaking only of the formal courses: university itself was life-changing. It's probably always been true that you have to find your way through or around formal education in the search for what really matters. You don't have to call it 'the meaning of life' and, after Monty Python's film of that name, you'd have to be brave to do so. (Then again, why not?) Philosophy at Keele was especially disappointing. It was the era of Oxford-dominated 'ordinary language' philosophy. In this kind of philosophy, it takes the first year at least to kill off the natural philosopher in a young person, by which I mean that part of them which combines a dissatisfaction with life on the one hand with a great curiosity about it, on the other, and most important of all, a profoundly naïve but essentially correct sense of its unlimited, unrealized, potential. Which leads them to ask questions about the Big Stuff, about the meaning of life. Once all that has been killed off, and the demoralized student made to concede that most Big Stuff questions are a waste of time (because meaningless), then he or she can be trained up in the arid discourse of analytic philosophy. With a couple of honourable and memorable exceptions (Brian Smart and John Grundy), the thing about the tutors I met at Keele is that they were seemingly born boring; I mean that in their cases nothing had to be killed off first – they never had been natural philosophers, but came nit-picking from the womb. Of course, most of them had also come from Oxford, the home of this kind of philosophy, and most were waiting for the call to return.

By the end of my first foundation year (Keele was then a four-year course), I knew I'd made a mistake and changed from philosophy to sociology. But one day in the department office, the philosophy tutor who had originally interviewed me sidled up and urged me to think again; I'd make rather a good philosopher he said. Although this didn't tally with the essay marks he'd given me, I was flattered and changed back to philosophy. Only later did I realize that I'd been persuaded to stay because the numbers in philosophy were very low that year. Second major lesson of higher education: duplicity flows both ways!

Of my time studying philosophy, three encounters now stand out. The first was the time Professor Anthony Flew threw me out of his room. I'd gone to complain about the syllabus. The handbook had promised that we would study philosophy from Plato to existentialism. In fact, there was no existentialism – and nothing on a great deal else.

'The fact is,' said Flew, and as he was talking he was crawling on the floor with his arse towards me, trying to recover papers that had fallen from his desk, 'existentialists aren't real philosophers. And anyway, the trouble with you young people today is that you always think the grass is greener on the other side of the hill.'

Now only a week or so before, I'd attended a lecture by Flew, who was in those days a reductive empiricist, on Johnson's refutation of Berkeley's idealism. Flew had told us how Johnson famously kicked a stone, uttering 'I refute him thus'. There in Flew's room, I had one of those transgressive impulses which are, at heart, purely ironic and aesthetic: I wanted to kick him up the arse, crying as I did so, 'I refute you thus!' I didn't, but he still threw me out.

The second event was when I fell out with Flew's successor, Professor Richard Swinburne, who has spent his academic life trying to prove the existence of God. I had led a student protest to his door, complaining that he'd allowed his religious views to prejudice his marking of our essays on the topic of abortion. By chance we'd come across what I think was then a relatively new publication called *Philosophy and Public Affairs* and, in particular, an article which argued that, according to certain criteria of aliveness, it was more immoral to kill a calf than a human infant of the same age. That did not go down at all well with Swinburne's own Christian commitments and he suggested I cease attending his seminars. I remember thinking – unfortunately too late as a parting shot – that if I were God and someone like Swinburne proved my existence I'd probably kill myself.

The third encounter involved the philosophy tutor who had interviewed me. It was at a finals party. A friend and I had wrapped ourselves in bedsheets and presented ourselves as Socrates and Alcibiades. The tutor, pretending not to notice our attire, asked me if I had considered going on to do post-grad work in the subject. I ran a mile. Swinburne eventually got the call back to Oxford, where he continued his Divine Mission, while Flew, who spent most of his philosophical life denying the existence of God, supposedly changed his mind shortly before he died. As for the philosopher who interviewed me, I've never heard of him again.

Not surprisingly, then, I looked for inspiration outside of the Philosophy department. I read other things, especially those anthologies of existentialism that discovered that everyone interesting in the European tradition was a proto-existentialist, with titles like 'Existentialism from Shakespeare to Jaspers'. In fact, I read Jaspers in great awe, after being told (probably erroneously) that his teaching of nihilism was so compelling that his students regularly committed suicide. Now there, I thought, was a real philosopher! To this day, if I think of those philosophers who have most influenced me, few, if any, have been 'real' philosophers in Professor Flew's sense of the term. And before I name some of them, let me say what I mean by 'influence': as well as the obvious sense of the word, I mean these are writers who I have lived with, returned to, learned from hesitantly and piecemeal, for as long as I've been reading. That it takes that long is a consequence of their intelligence and my limitations as a thinker. The limitations of the recipient are a neglected aspect of influence, not least because to succumb to one kind of influence is to turn away from others. But you have to find your own way. So, of those who have influenced me here's a few: Ecclesiastes, Seneca, Montaigne, Schopenhauer, Nietzsche, Marx and Freud. I don't know what might connect them unless it be this: in very different ways all see human consciousness as alienated from the very reality which it strives to understand and for some of them that alienation becomes intrinsic to human desire. In a hesitant and incompetent way, I was discovering back then that philosophy was not only more important than the academic study of it allowed, but that as a subject it needed to be turned against the academy which diminished it. That became the basis of everything I subsequently wrote, and if it has had any merit, it's because it grew out of a deep dissatisfaction with the way the academic world smothered, tamed and domesticated the subjects it controlled.

# 3

# Life-changing wager, 1977

I've started a job at the University of Sussex. On my way home in the evenings, I sometimes stop off at the student bar, a popular meeting place for other faculty as well as students.

On this particular evening, I find there one of my students, Duncan, and he introduces me to another, older student, P (he's asked me not to use his full name). I know Duncan is gay and it soon becomes clear P is too. I'm curious. P is provocative – he has a wicked sense of humour, is sometimes camp but edgily so and delights in being outrageous. I'm intrigued at the way he doesn't seem to care whether or not he actually believes what he says, although I guess that he does believe some things quite strongly. He came to England from the West Indies only a few years earlier, initially training as a nurse but then deciding he wanted to go to university. He and I are the same age. I sense he's quite dangerous, though as yet I can't say why. I later learn he'd made a bet with Duncan that day in the bar that he could get me into bed.

P invites me around to his bedsit. It's very small – there's only space for a single bed – but neat. There's nothing of interest to describe but every detail of it fascinates me, including the old record player on the floor on which he introduces to me Van Morrison's 'Madame George'. We don't drink much and are soon on the single bed together. I have no misgivings about this. I'd realized I'm bisexual for a few years at least, but my homosexuality has felt more latent than anything, with no very strong desire for gay experience. I know I enjoy looking at beautiful young men, especially when that beauty suggests someone who is alive sensually, never having been attracted to the merely pretty. Beauty without sensuality, in both genders, leaves me indifferent; likewise, with the immaculately dressed, especially those for whom style substitutes for, or conceals a lack of, sensuality. But with young men, this looking has until now been passive: I am happy enough to just gaze and seem by no means alone in this. If popular culture is anything to go by, it would appear the whole world is gazing at young male beauty, even more so than female. No misgivings then, and much curiosity ...

What sex we have on this first encounter isn't great, mainly down to my inexperience, but this doesn't seem to worry P at all, and we lay awake for most of the night, up close in this single bed, talking. We become intimate, finding we can talk to each other about anything and everything, and by the morning we've become unexpectedly close. It feels as if he could become to me a brother in ways my actual brothers never have been. But I still have no idea that this could become a relationship. Over the next few days, I find myself thinking about him as someone I want to be with, not least because he makes me laugh. But there's something else: P is a conflicted mix of the anarchic and the moral, the wilful and the thoughtful and time with him is never boring. This is attractive to me.

Academic life was already becoming tedious in some respects and I'd barely started out on my 'career'. That's probably why there's little in this narrative about academia. Much of it seemed at the time, and still seems, unmemorable, unremarkable, boring, as our day jobs so often are. And while the scholarship of the books I wrote was learned inside the university, their inspiration came from outside. The life episodes in this memoir are those which interest me as a writer, some of them helping me become one.

> And, of course, my erotic interest is growing. We are definitely drawn to each other, we meet some more, and inevitably fall into bed again, and P patiently, and expertly, teaches me about gay sex and I like what I'm learning. I imagine all sex which begins in visual attraction to be in some way aesthetic, while supposing, too, that at some stage the visual gaze eventually dissolves into sensation and, ultimately, the blind intensity of orgasm. One of the things I am discovering is that, for me, the dissolution of the gaze is later in gay than in straight sex, sometimes staying right through: holding eye contact to the end, the intense appreciation of beauty is now part of the pleasure. There's something else: sometimes in gay sex I find there's a way in which his desire becomes the focus of my desire, and in a way which is subtly different from wanting to give pleasure, or wanting him to desire me, although both those things may be its consequence. Rather his desire becomes an aspect of his beauty, and elicits from me an erotic attention different again from wanting to have or to possess. As I write this, I wonder if my same-sex desire will strike some as absurdly cerebral or aesthetic, but that's just how it is. Anyhow, it couldn't have been *that* cerebral because all this means is that one night, P and I fuck each other; I have no idea it can be this ecstatic and there's no going back.

The classic legal definition of obscenity, going back to the mid-nineteenth century, refers to what can 'deprave and corrupt those whose minds are open to such immoral influences'. It's customary for the sophisticated, 'liberated' modernist to sneer at this, but I think there's a sense in which those paranoid Victorian legislators got it exactly right in their awareness, or dread, of how potentially 'open' the human animal is to erotic influence. Of course, they were referring to the effect of publications, which has been magnified a thousandfold with the prevalence of pornography on the internet. When it comes down to the active seduction of one person by another, the potential to influence and change (deprave and corrupt) is compounded by at least another thousandfold (my numbers here are arbitrary). My point is that I wasn't exceptional in being 'open' to the influence of P any more than of Tony, and whether it's called corruption or initiation, depravity or education, ruin or liberation is to me irrelevant.

For a while, I came to believe this proved that desire was all a question of culture not nature: how else to explain such a dramatic change in myself? But obviously it isn't, and I now feel there is always, or should be, something mysterious about desire. If you look at the way most people live, human desire can seem amazingly compliant with the history of our culture and, more immediately, with our specific socialization, so much so that it comes to seem nothing but their creation. To borrow a metaphor from the seventeenth-century philosopher John Locke, it's as if desire begins as a *tabula rasa* which then has the social script written upon it (that script being, until recently, heterosexuality, marriage, monogamy, etc.) Conversely, desire can also be so intransigently, perversely, resistant to history and socialization, that the opposite seems equally plausible, namely that the real force of desire is rooted in a pre-social instinct or libido. How else, for instance, to explain P becoming, and knowing, he was, homosexual from an early age in society that was so homophobic as to make it, culturally speaking, unthinkable as a life option?

If something is the effect of nature rather than nurture then, so the argument goes, it can't be changed and nor should we try to change it. This was the claim of some in the early decades of gay liberation, against those who thought homosexuality was the effect of depraving and corrupting influence and therefore could and should be be corrected. However, history also teaches us that sometimes the most recalcitrant kind of desire is not natural at all, but that which we know to be the effect of prolonged socialization. Especially today: maybe in the foreseeable future it will be easier or quicker to genetically alter human nature than to change certain aspects of human cultures. And what about those like me, who grew up desiring and thinking in the prescribed ways, but for various reasons become open to new kinds of desire? In the world of my childhood, homosexuality was despised and demonized. When I first started work in the factory, I didn't have a girlfriend, and when at a tea break one of the other apprentices said jokingly that I'd need to get one soon or people would start thinking I was queer, I was plunged into a humiliating despair which lasted for weeks. I'm sure – I hope – I wanted a girlfriend for other and better reasons, too, but from that moment on all that mattered was that I procure one to prove I wasn't queer.

It wasn't until I started to study Western literature and philosophy, and in particular the Greeks (which I took as a subsidiary subject at university) that I learned about the history of homosexuality, its prevalence in ours and other cultures. Learning about it didn't just help me acknowledge my own bisexuality, it helped create and form it, too. This has also happened to countless others, most of whom lived in far less tolerant times. Acknowledging or exploring one's homosexuality today isn't the problem it once was, of course, nor was it that big a deal when it happened for me in the 1970s. It's true that it had only been decriminalized a decade before, and that when I came out to my father he did briefly threaten to disinherit me, but since he had precisely nothing to leave this wasn't exactly a hardship. But imagine writing home about this from college in the 1950s, when homosexuality was still illegal; it's a letter I'd dearly loved to have written:

Dear Mum and Dad,
So glad you persuaded me to do the Great Books course. I find I just love high culture; the Greeks especially are terrific, and studying them has made me realize I'm just, well, so Uranian. I've found a sturdy little chum called Dorian, and I'll be bringing him home for Christmas.
Your ever-loving son, etc.

With me something else was happening, too: in a much more general way, education was giving me the language and the reasons to be critical of the dominant culture and ideology, the doxa, and to realize that often the deviant and the dissenting, the marginal and the subordinate are just so much more interesting – certainly less boring. So I actively started to explore and embrace what my upbringing had condemned as corrupt or depraved. Or, to put the same point rather more respectably, if learning doesn't make us less obedient, it's probably failed. Homoerotic desire came to fascinate me because of the way it has moved between cultural extremes which aren't unique to it but which, for historical reason, it has experienced and recorded with particular intensity: now deeply nostalgic, preoccupied with transience and loss, now passionately affirmative and utopian; now politically responsive and humanely responsible, now anarchically dissident.

So, if I try to explain how P and me ended up in that single bed in Brighton, well, at one level it's obvious: he had a bet to win and I was my usual curious self, staving off tedium and hungry for new experience. But if I think about how and why we went on to fall in love, all I can say for sure is that it was mysterious and paradoxical: our mutual attraction was at once a consequence of our hugely different histories, and a refusal of those same histories. But I *was* in love. At the time I wasn't reading much, but one book I did read was about the great opposites of life – love and hate, health and sickness, good and evil, life and death, etc. – and how artists and philosophers discover they are not really opposites at all, but fatally interconnected. I remember scrawling in the margin something like: 'and the lover, while in love, prises the opposites apart again, for just as long as he's in love'.

At the time, I was in a long-term relationship with a woman who I also loved, but in a very different way. When I told her what was happening between me and P, it ended that relationship. I hurt her and to this day I am sorry for that. At the time, I told her I didn't expect to have a relationship with

P; I just felt a need to be up front about what was happening; she asked me to choose, and I chose him, although at the time I felt as if I had no choice, even though I didn't expect anything to last with P. As it happened, it did last for a while: we were together for about a year.

# Sex and the self

Still, I found my experience didn't fit the narratives that my new-found gay friends were offering to make sense of it. I've lived through a time of increasing convergence of self and sexuality. Most obviously it's the basis of the sexual liberation movements – not exactly the conflation of self and sexuality, but the making of the latter an essential truth of the former. So, for some liberationists, the claim would go something like this: I am not just someone who happens to be gay, rather my homosexuality is one of the most important thing about me – perhaps the most important – and I cannot be myself without the freedom to express my sexuality. Repress that and you stultify me. Allow me to be gay and you allow me to be who I essentially am. It's sometimes called identity politics, and there's a residue – more than that – of Western spirituality in it, and it's no surprise that in recent years it has been so prevalent in the Church of England, even to the point of threatening to split it apart.

I've never felt that my sexuality is the true expression of myself. For a start the self is elusive: what exists is consciousness and desire, both of which, if they can be understood at all can only be done so in relation to what they are not – *what* am I conscious of, *what* is it I desire? – and even then only fleetingly. Moreover, identity is inherently unstable. Philosophers tell us that it is determined by spatio-temporal continuity, which is, of course, consistent with total change (a thing remains the same thing even if every part of it has been replaced, one after another, across a certain period).

More significantly, sexuality at its most intense has often thrown me into confusion; the compulsion, the vulnerability of sex sometimes threatening the/my self. Bluntly, I have found that I can be wrecked by desire to an extent which puts 'me' deeply into question. Other people 'come out' as who they *really* are, but for me sexual desire confuses, undermines or at least alters my sense of self. In a way the promise of change is always there, constantly repeated, in the way orgasm momentarily obliterates the self and, when the confusion of desire clarifies, the always present possibility that what reappears is an altered self. It's sometimes called falling in love, and falling into, or towards, something presupposes leaving something else. So, when I embarked on this first gay affair with P I didn't feel as if I had at last become my true self. If classification is necessary then I was, and remain, bisexual. There was some pressure from political gay culture for me to acknowledge that I had discovered my true (gay) self, but I hadn't – not exactly. I didn't fit a classic gay coming out narrative; in other words, I had not at last become the person I'd always really been. On the contrary, almost overnight, as it were, it felt as if I had become a different person. This wasn't so much a self-discovery as a bewildering, exhilarating, radical transformation of the self. I was going to say 'self-transformation', but that wouldn't be right either, because it felt like a transformation of the self by something other than the self, by *desire*. It's one of the delusions of identity politics to think that our desire comfortably coexists with our identity, a belief which has to do more with consumerism than desire. I've come to feel that sexuality might at different times express different aspects of one's self, a situation further complicated by the fact that the self changes. I suppose this is most obviously the case with bisexuality because it crosses between different categories, but it may be true more generally: sexuality not as a single unified drive but different ones, corresponding to different aspects of oneself, or of a changing self – aspects which may well be in conflict or at least sometimes be so different as to be able to talk of different sexual selves.

The bisexual has been distrusted by both straights and gays, who demand to know what he or she *really* is, or at least which side is the more dominant. In my own case that's difficult to answer: a common sense or identity politics view might conclude that what one really *is* corresponds to that sex towards which one feels a straightforward attraction or desire. So, if, in an uncomplicated way, I'm attracted to women more than men I'm mainly straight; if men, I'm mainly gay. But again, that doesn't work for me: I think one's sexuality corresponds to the sex in relation to which one also feels *complication*: loss, distress, confusion, ecstasy, abjection, because these things are intrinsic to love, to desire. To be alive is to desire and to desire is, sooner rather than later to be deeply, subjectively confused. And hurt: not just through the loss of the desired, but because, for me, desire at its most intense seems to be pressured by an obscure, distantly past hurt, irretrievable to consciousness, yet remembered viscerally, somewhere in my being. Birth, maybe?

At times, I know I am far more homosexual that heterosexual because it's homosexual desire that hurts, that has the potential to wreck me. But at earlier times in my life it's been heterosexual desire which has had that potential. Is there such a thing as uncomplicated, straightforward sex? Of course. But it's not love, it's not even desire. Desire is always potentially dangerous because you never quite know when it is going to subvert selfhood, reveal it as the fiction or fabrication that it is; 'fabrication' because it is a construct susceptible to unravelling, coming to pieces. Sometimes in life, and commonly in literature, desire undermines our resolve, drives us to obsession, illness, madness, or even death; or splits us into self-division, or contradictory moral evaluation, or wrecks us with the ambivalence of love and hate fused in the same desire. And perhaps the most resonant complication occurs when the threat to self-hood is embraced: I assume I'm not alone in being ambivalent about identity, the desire to consolidate it being haunted by an equally powerful desire to relinquish it.

Some of that at least was going on with P and me. In very different ways, we each bought some difficult histories to the relationship, those of race and class, among others, and we were both conflicted and confused and fought a lot. Also we were both reckless, keen to explore and push desire to the point where it subverted identity. At the same time, P wanted acceptance in the culture he'd arrived into and initially sex seemed one way to achieve that, especially given that he was attractive and the opportunities numerous. Very soon though he encountered the stereotypes of blacks in white gay culture, which made him deeply ambivalent about his place inside it. When he related to me some of his experiences on first connecting with that culture in London, I was reminded of what James Baldwin had written about his own sexual encounters in New York in the 1940s:

> Sometimes, eventually, inevitably, I would find myself in bed with one of these men, a despairing and dreadful conjunction, since their need was as relentless as quicksand and as impersonal, and sexual rumour concerning blacks had preceded me ... At bottom what I had learned was that the male desire for a male roams everywhere, avid, desperate, unimaginably lonely, culminating often in drugs, piety, madness or death. It was also dreadfully like watching myself at the end of a long, slow moving line: Soon I would be next. All of this was very frightening. It was lonely, and impersonal and demeaning. I could not believe after all, I was only nineteen that I could have been driven to the lonesome place where these men and I met each other so soon, to stay. (*The Price of the Ticket*)

Those who find this a too pessimistic view of homosexual desire also move too quickly to explaining it in terms of the oppressiveness and discrimination of the time. But that line – 'sexual rumour concerning blacks had preceded me' – was in some respects just as true for P as a West Indian immigrant encountering the gay subculture of 1970s' London. Even in the more 'refined' quarters of that culture, it remained an issue: he could have become the kept partner of any one of a number of rich gay men, but he knew he was better than that; it was one reason why he was at university. But for someone who had known difficult times these weren't easy choices, especially since he was also insecure about his academic abilities, unjustifiably so as it turned out, later training as a psychotherapist.

For my part, I was guilty of some double standards – I wanted this relationship to last, but I also wanted to play the gay scene for all it was worth and I went to it with the passion of the recent convert. My first encounter with the gay scene was when P took me to the Curtain Club in Brighton. I loved it there, and especially I loved being the object of sexual attention, it all being new to me. P was by then experienced on the scene, and tried to curtail my enthusiasm, but I was having none of it. I remember him saying once, in exasperation, that I was like a puppy wanting to play, falling into step, with anyone who gave it attention, and he was right. Partly because I was a new face on the scene, partly because I was with P, and partly because I was a biker, I did get some attention, and it fed my narcissism, which, while not insatiable, was hungry enough. I wouldn't generalize about this, and anyway things have changed in this respect since, but, back then, the straight women I'd known in my life weren't, initially at least, into their men as physically as gay men were into each other. To be desired by another man, at least on the gay scene, was to be desired in a shamelessly physical way. You knew what they wanted – though not always *precisely* what they wanted to do with or to you – and to begin with it was flattering. Something else: it's no secret that gay male cruising culture is obsessed with youth, and in that context I found I could always pass as younger than I was, right up to my early forties. I also pretended to myself that the hedonism of gay culture was the answer to the recurring depression which had haunted me for at least a decade by then. I told myself that I hadn't lived enough, that all I needed to do was seize the night a bit more zealously and I could shake off the darkness. It was naïve, of course, as was my inclination, when I sensed that this wasn't working, to try even harder.

For these, and other reasons, too, our relationship foundered. In fact, it ended so badly that we didn't speak to each other again for about six years. But I never stopped loving P and I part-dedicated my first book to him, a book for which, indirectly, yet importantly, he was partly responsible. Characteristically, he trashed me for not giving him sole dedication, but eventually we started up a friendship again, something was still alive between us and we became close once more, and to this day remain so.

Shortly after we separated, I began to have dreams about another road accident, this time one that I'd indirectly caused.

# Broken bodies

My current motorbike is a Honda 500/4 which I've just fitted with a new four-into-one exhaust system. It now howls, with a delicious edge to the sound which sharpens, or hardens, as the revs rise. The sound of an engine revved sympathetically to near (not beyond) its limit, is for me as seductive as speed itself. On my way across Brighton to P's flat, I round a corner fast and then accelerate hard along a short straight going uphill. I know the road and that I can get the bike to around 70mph if I hold off the braking until the last minute. There's a man on the pavement on my side of the road who stops to watch me pass. In my handle-bar mirror, I watch him watching me, not sure if he's admiring or disapproving, and not much caring which, holding the bike in second up to the red line. The sound is, as always, delicious, reverberating back off adjacent buildings. But then, just as I start to brake, still watching a receding, vibrating image of the man watching me, he steps into the path of a van. He doesn't go under its wheels, but is thrown up into the air and maybe hit a second time by the top of the windscreen. I pull up, turn the bike around and ride back towards him until about 50 yards away and stop. His body is crumpled, lying awkwardly. How badly broken I don't know. A woman is dabbing his face with some kind of cloth. The van driver is kneeling down, too, and another car is also stopping nearby. I know that indirectly I've been the cause of the accident. After watching for a few moments, I turn the bike around and head for P's place. I'm not sure why, but I don't tell him about the accident. He wants to make love as soon as I arrive, which we do, and I still have the image of that crumpled body in my mind. At first it's inhibiting, but as I get more aroused it gives me a heightened sense of P's physical beauty.

That was a couple of months ago. Shortly after that P and I part. In the last couple of nights, I've had dreams of P's body, broken and crumpled on a road I don't know, can't identify.

So now, on my own, as curious as ever, yet still the relative new comer to gay culture, I went cruising, oblivious of the dangers that awaited. As I did so, as I shared other beds, I always remembered P's single one, and, usually, in the same memory, a poem by Cavafy called 'The Afternoon Sun': 'Beside the window the bed; / the afternoon sun fell across half of it'.

# 4

# New York: City of many Sirens

## The Saint, 1982

We're sitting on the top floor of the Saint nightclub in the East Village. It's dark up here, less so at the front, which gets some of the light from the floor below, more so at the back, which is where men are having sex.

I'm here with Peter, someone I met a couple of weeks ago, and with whom I'm now staying. He lives nearby in one of those old corridor apartments near St Mark's Place. It's run down and full of cockroaches, which come out at dusk. Peter used to be a classics scholar at an American University, but left voluntarily because he hated it. Now he works nights doing something connected with printing. He's around forty, eccentric and hippie looking: long hair, full beard and seriously wrong clothes for a chic club like this. I like him: he's socially gauche, brutally honest and very intelligent. And lonely. We've been talking casually, on and off, about Greek tragedy, philosophers he admires, why he got out of the university.

This is a seductive place, an old theatre converted at (I assume) great expense into a gay club on three floors. The light and sound systems are spectacular. The first floor is a

huge bar area; the second a dance floor whose roof is a kind
of planetarium, and the top floor, where we are – the former
theatre circle – is the sex room. I'm restless and eventually
tell Peter I'm going to join the fray. He's fine with that,
tells me to be safe and stays where he is, drinking, smoking
and observing in a detached, non-voyeuristic way which
is how I always remember him. I join a group of men and
soon one of them is blowing me, another kissing me and a
third is doing other definitely unsafe things. Actually there
may be a fourth and a fifth, but by now I'm not sure and it
doesn't matter. I feel someone's cock in my hand and draw
it to me; it fucks me slowly but still I can't hold off coming
and, as I do so, I notice that the guy blowing me makes
sure nothing that issues forth messes up his (presumably)
designer clothes.

After retrieving my own clothes, I find a toilet and clean
up before going back to join Peter. He's in the same place
and we resume the conversation where we left off. 'I tell
you to be safe and I'm guessing you went and did just the
opposite' he says, with quiet exasperation. I smile, in a
hopefully disarming way, and he shrugs. There's increasing
talk of some kind of nasty illness here, which may or may
not be sexually transmitted. I first heard about it a few weeks
back in New Orleans, where there was some speculation,
but not much hard evidence. One rumour is that it's related
to the use of amyl, but that doesn't seem to be stopping
anyone here. Anyhow, with sex out of the way, I feel even
happier and we talk for a long while in a way which both
is intimate and honest without being indulgent. I've found
many conversations in this city are coercively and dishon-
estly intimate. Each of us is interested in, and has decided
to trust, the other. I ask Peter why he's so ruthlessly honest
with people, and whether he cares that it loses him friends
or at least makes people keep their distance. He shrugs,
then after a moment or two tells me that for him being
honest makes living more interesting, adding, 'usually more
so than this', gesturing to the sex going on around us. After

a while, he says something else that stays with me; it was one of those remarks that seems at once so enlightening as to be potentially life-changing, and yet so plausible as to be obvious: 'Besides, if the truth hurts, you're probably living all wrong; your life is probably a lie.' With that, we fall silent and watch the shadowy figures at the back, also silent apart from the odd groan or gasp. And once, a yelp.

An hour or so later we separate and I fall into conversation with a group I'd briefly seen earlier, while queuing to get into the club. As I and others waited in the cold, a stretch-limo had drawn up and this group, about seven in all, got out, went straight to the head of the queue and were promptly admitted. As one of them passed, he looked at me and asked flatly: 'Are you cold?' I replied that I was, which was stupid, because almost before I had opened my mouth he was looking through me with an expression of indifference, as if he'd already forgotten he'd asked the question. It was this man who I was talking to now. He told me his name but I've forgotten it. I'll call him Successful. He hasn't recognized me from the earlier encounter and started talking to me when he heard me ordering a drink. It was small talk; vanity talk. He tells me about the (very successful) business he runs and some of the famous people he knows and then takes me upstairs to the dance floor. He points out some notable people, including an ordinary looking guy who was, apparently, both a noted writer – I hadn't heard of him – and one of the most in-demand rent boys in the city.

'Writes like an angel and hung like a horse', Successful tells me. He reels off some names of other famous people 'in tonight', the only one of which I vaguely recognize is Mapplethorpe.

It's about 3 a.m. and the frenzy on the dance floor is building. There must be at least 2,000 people on the floor, a seething mass of energy like a great tidal wave, endlessly dissolving back into itself and going nowhere. The air is thick with amyl. The dancing climaxes with a huge mirrored sphere, a kind of sun, descending from the planetarium roof. As it does so, Successful puts his arm around my shoulders and says: 'You know, everyone in New York is young, beautiful and rich.'

I look at him. He's clearly high on something, but by no means wasted: an elegant cocktail, the kind which allows you to maintain poise. I could just about go along with the young and beautiful fantasy, but rich as well? What's that about? I can't help myself: not out of indignation, but rather sheer curiosity as to his way of thinking, I say: 'That's not how it strikes me.'

With only slight difficulty, he focuses on me, looks puzzled and asks what I mean. Now feeling rather awkward, I nevertheless follow through: 'Well, there're a lot of derelict people on the streets out there.' He thinks for a bit, nods and then replies, with not a trace of irony, annoyance or sarcasm: 'Well, I guess they just don't know the right people.'

Peter also takes me to the local St Marks bathhouse which, I discover, is owned by the same guy who operates the Saint. The bathhouse strikes me as more honest than the club, maybe because people talk less here. I'm drawn to the graffiti on the walls of its cubicles: 'Pete loves Jonnie. For a day'; 'Masochism Rules'; 'A Thing of Beauty is a Boy Forever'. Most things are happening, including S&M, fist-fucking, with others watching, among whom is a couple affectionately holding hands as they do so. The exhibitionism is truly naked, and all this in an earnest, dedicated silence; it's one of the intriguing ironies of human sexuality that it can get ugly in its obsession with human beauty, but not here, at least not tonight: it's ritualized, stylized, self-conscious theatre. In one cubicle, a youth is lying face down, languidly waiting to be fucked. By anyone. Further along I discover Peter in a clinch with someone I thought I recognized. I did: it was a guy who had blown me in the Saint some nights before. I leave them to it but not before noticing the guy had his designer clothes with him, neatly folded on the floor. I settle for some tame sex with a man who, I soon learn, loves – and only loves – giving head. He tells me he will happily spend the whole night there servicing anyone who comes along, except those with excessively large dicks. These he avoids if he can because they give him jaw ache. He tells me this is in a matter of fact way, seemingly unaware, or unconcerned that it might be detrimental to the fantasy life of the place.

Earlier that day, waiting for the nightlife to begin, I'd been reading Thomas Mann and thinking again about his intense, homoerotic yearning and the speculation about what, if any, actual homosexual experience he'd had. No one really knows, but it's possible it was very little; clasping the odd boy to his chest may have been about it. He was typical of the bourgeois writer, living prudentially, yet fascinated by excess, or as Flaubert puts it, be regular and orderly in your life so that you may be violent and original in your work. That night, in the bathhouse, as I pass someone being fucked too hard, I suddenly find myself thinking: what if Mann – or Flaubert, for that matter – were here, witnessing all his? Given that Mann's art was a sustained, conscious sublimation of his largely unrequited, fantasized yearning, what would he have made of it? Had all this been available to him, would his writing have been radically different? Might he have joined in? Starting at the vanilla end of what was on offer and moving up to the more extreme stuff, that being what frequent visitors to these places sometimes do? And might he have stopped writing as a consequence? (Those who can, do, those who can't, write – Faulkner.) Or maybe he would just have fled in terror and kept writing. I wouldn't have blamed him if he had – fled I mean. Human sexuality isn't essentially or inevitably daemonic but it has this potential to become so, often when we least expect it. It doesn't even have to be daemonic to be shocking. I later shared these thoughts with another new-found friend familiar with the New York scene and he mocked be for being a scene-virgin. I still think that anyone who claims to be unshockable by human sexuality, even its extremes, is either lying or hasn't understood it or themselves, or both. That's true of writers, too. You can read any number of accounts of extreme sexuality where the narrative voice depicting them is implicitly saying: this will hopefully shock you but it doesn't shock me. Usually it's a fraudulent voice – and in more ways than one. I read somewhere that even sexual psychopaths are capable of being shocked by a sexuality not their own. I don't pathologise or judge sexual extremists, but nor have I found I can quite trust their own account of what they think they are doing.

Some years later, when I'd learned more about philosopher Michel Foucault's own discovery of the US gay scene, I thought often about what it had meant to him, how profoundly it had affected *his* writing, as well as putting a premature end to it. I assume it was here that he contracted the HIV virus which contributed to his death in 1984, at around the same time, I realize, that I was exploring the scene in New York, although I believe he mainly frequented the West Coast gay scene. So sadly, our paths probably never crossed. But then, given the lighting in some of those places, I doubt if I'd have recognized him even if they had.

This year (2014) a friend, Michael, and I are travelling in France and decide to visit Foucault's grave in the small town of Vendeuvre-du-Poitou, where he also grew up. We find the graveyard easily enough but can't find the grave. There's an elderly man nearby, tending the grave of his recently deceased wife and, after a fruitless search, we ask him for assistance. He's lived in the town all his life and knows of Foucault; he confirms that he is buried in this graveyard, but doesn't know where. He helps us look but again with no success. So Michael and I head off to the local Mairie; surely they will know? They don't, not immediately, but they do recall that someone else had once come by looking for a grave of that name. Clearly the town isn't capitalizing on its famous philosopher inhabitant. Anyhow, they examine their records and eventually find a plan which seems to show Foucault's grave. We return with a map and at last find it. We talk again to the same man and he tells us that as a boy Foucault was regarded with suspicion because there was 'the smell of Sulphur about him' and, on one occasion, Foucault's mother had confessed to his own mother that she didn't know what was going to become of him. Walking around that quiet, small town, I try to imagine how alienated from it Foucault must have felt – certainly because of his homosexuality, but for other reasons, too; biographers record that his childhood here wasn't a happy one. Later, when we are looking at the house where Foucault's family lived, a man stops to ask if he can help us. On learning that we are interested in Michel Foucault, he gives us the fleeting, knowing look of someone who is clandestinely gay and who assumes we are also, this being the reason why we're interested in one of the town's more notorious inhabitants.

So the child who grew up in a small, conservative town in France becomes famous, and it's fame which takes him to the US West Coast, where he ends up revelling in the gay backrooms of San Francisco, finding in sadomasochistic sex what he called a 'limit experience', a potentially radical kind of pleasure that might challenge the oppressive norms of our culture, sexual and otherwise. There were others who claimed, less extremely and more plausibly, that the gay club/sex scene was radically egalitarian; or that the high of the gay disco was a utopian experience, where resistance to the oppressions of race and homosexuality met and merged with a hope of a different and freer future, for both gays and blacks, a hope tragically destroyed by HIV/AIDS. At the time, I wanted to believe some of that at least, but, by the late 1980s, any such belief had gone, and the encounter with Successful in the Saint, was, I now see, a decisive moment in my scepticism.

Once, on my way home in the morning after a night out in London, I passed the club we'd been in and, on impulse, went in. It was around 10 a.m. and mainly immigrant workers were just starting to clean the place. They went about their work with the purposeful, mindless insularity which helps time pass and which I remembered from the factory, and I wandered around unchallenged. Under the glare of ordinary lighting, all I could see was the hideous tackiness of the decor, the debris of excess and indulgence including bottles, glasses, spilt alcohol, empty amyl capsules, a needle, vomit and the dried stains of what were probably bodily fluids.

Sometimes the sordidness of the back room was striking enough to be visible even in the dark. A haunt I found in Gran Canaria was typical. To get to it you go from the bustling shopping centre, with its tourists and families, into a bar, much like any other, except that there're only men, drinking and cruising. Then, off this bar is the video room where other men are drinking, smoking, silently watching pornographic movies of young men in interminable sequences of sucking or fucking each other: no plot; zero fantasy. Occasionally, someone slips into or leaves the last room of all, the back room. It's small, even by back room standards, and just dark enough to make people look more attractive than they actually are. Later, the floor is slippery with spent come, condoms and spilt drink. Before going in, if you don't conceal your money in a sock or shoe, you'll lose it. Are those who lift it thieves passing as gay, or are they gay thieves? Either way, they'll almost certainly be having sex at the moment they take it. By the time I get in there I'm half wasted and forget to hide mine, and the guy who is blowing me takes it all, proving to be as deft of hand as he was of mouth. In fact, by my calculations he definitely must have had a third hand, and I'm impressed, but also annoyed because this isn't the first time this has happened and I should know better. Also I'm some miles from my hotel with nothing for a taxi back. Fortunately, I get picked up by someone with a car. He's unmemorable apart from accidentally (I hope) spilling a full bottle of amyl over us both, when we're naked.

So no, there was nothing politically radical about those clubs or back rooms. Their ethos was much the same as most other city haunts across the years (centuries?), haunts with sexual and other kinds of pleasure on offer and seized by people typically at once frenetic yet distracted, avaricious yet tired. What I experienced in the Saint in New York, and in other clubs in Western cities, was commercialized decadence through and through, a well-heeled hedonism which, because it was dominated by codes of chic, fashion and the in-crowd, was conformist even in its excesses. It sneered at those who fell short appearance-wise, assuming they had the courage to be seen there at all – and mostly they didn't. Above and beneath all of it was a slavish obsession with physical beauty, and a pathetically narrow conception of what constituted it at that. The irony, of course, is that it all seemed so safe and reassuring: sex here was not the shuddering surrender to some overwhelming desire whose intensity was the greater for its previous repression, but the expression of something domes-ticated, controlled, commodified and tamed, an exercise of consumer choice rather than daemonic compulsion.

For sure, the sexual freedom on offer was new and remarkable, and nowhere did it quite like the gay scene in New York, city of so many Sirens. The Saint was only in operation for about seven years, but it became a legend; at its height it claimed to be the most fabulous club in the world, and I suspect it probably was. Like so many others, I was drawn to such clubs and took risks with the easy sex on offer. But just as much, I loved the way the throb of the disco music entered and melted you, the way it passed right through you, seductively embracing your libido on the way, *from the inside*, and, with the help of the lighting and the drugs, caressing your fantasies, gently massaging you into an attitude of abandon, or a readiness for sexual abandon. They could also be places of adventure, or where adventure began, with the unexpected sometimes emerging from the predictable. As I write, there's growing media coverage of the popularity of so-called chemsex on the contemporary London gay scene. The drugs currently available seem even more seductive and potent than those of decades past, but the dilemmas are recognizably similar: of those who try them some become addicted and get destroyed, usually sooner rather than later; others eventually walk away, having learned something from them and never forgetting the early highs, and perhaps never feeling quite so alive again. Yet others are tempted, but abstain, as much for the wrong reasons as the right, and remain sensibly abstinent for the rest of their lives. Some aren't even tempted and these are among the least interesting people I've known.

I assume the human vulnerability to addiction is a complex mix of the genetic, the psychic and the social. For some, addiction has its origins in life-affirming impulses inseparable from that vulnerability, and it's these I remember as in a way tragic: addiction as the destiny, the irresistible betrayal, of vulnerable, life-affirming impulses. From my own experience, the recovering addict is in a permanent low-level state of unrequited desire. It's not just desire for something I can't have but for something which couldn't requite the desire even if I could. Somewhere at the very beginning of the fall into addiction there may have been, briefly, an experience of the perfect high, but it's more likely that the high was itself an experience of potential, of heightened desire for something newly realized but still, tantalizingly, just out of reach. That anyway is what addiction becomes. As addicts, we're trying to retrieve something that never quite existed in the form in which it's being lusted after. To say addiction, be it to sex or drugs, is self-destructive is simplistic; rather eventual ruin through hedonism is never surprising because always half anticipated; not because ruin is what was being sought, but because it was the recklessly entertained risk which seemed, at the time, the price of the adventure which beckoned.

When I first read the following passage from Oscar Moore's *A Matter of Life and Sex,* I couldn't share in friends' disapproval of it; for me there could be no judgement, only the thrill of recognition:

And there, locked in a backroom bathroom he had thrown himself into the clinch of sex with the smile of one preparing his last fix. There, in the stream of sweat and hallucination of amyl ... as the man's penis swelled and loomed ... and Hugo's mouth and eyes drooled in one gasping hunger, a quiet voice whispered – this could be the boy that kills you. And a quiet voice answered back – so then, this is the way to die.

That quiet voice is also an old voice, and heard in different registers. Freud quotes approvingly Groddeck's ponderous contention that: 'we are lived by unknown and uncontrollable forces', but the poets are the more perceptive, and when Graham Donaghy says: 'Though we command the language of desire / The voice of ecstasy is not our own', he's paraphrasing Yeats's 'Supernatural Songs':

> Eternity is passion, girl or boy
> Cry at the onset of their sexual joy
> 'For ever and for ever'; then awake
> Ignorant what Dramatis personae spake;
> A passion-driven exultant man sings out
> Sentences that he has never thought;
> The Flagellant lashes those submissive loins
> Ignorant what that dramatist enjoins,
> What master made the lash.

Perhaps most compelling, fatal and famous of all: the irresistible, seductive, voices of the Sirens, luring those who heard them to their death. But the sensible sceptics quite rightly remind me that it doesn't always have to be so extreme. They are right. Except that, even in the most mundane sexual encounter, we're initially attracted to each other in terms of the sensitively alive, daylight things – the eyes, the smile, the gesture – while in the embrace, the closer we come to ecstasy, the blinder we become to each other, and to ourselves: just for that brief, vulnerable moment of abandon. Though at the time we're usually too delirious to realize it, sexual abandon risks, even courts, self-annihilation if only in fantasy. Is that why, I find myself wondering, we mostly do it in the relative security of the bed? It's often said that each orgasm is a little death – la petite mort. It's also a little contradiction: the most intense experience the self can have is a temporary obliteration of self, and in this respect carnal ecstasy echoes its religious counterpart, unsurprisingly perhaps given that ecstasy was religious before it was sexual, although that was a time when it could also effortlessly embrace the sexual.

In clubs like the Saint, despite the mono-coolness of the culture, the compulsions, contradictions and dangers of desire did surface and I was fascinated by them when they did, and what they seemed to reveal about the mystery of human desire. When I think of the complexity of human erotic life and its diversity; of the mobility of our attachments, the unpredictability of our fantasies, the way sexuality can be both beautiful and ugly – ugly even or especially in its attraction to beauty; now sad, selfish and compulsive, now idealistic, selfless and rational; of the ways in which we make profoundly perverse identifications in the sexual imaginary; thinking of such things, which are only a glimpse of the full messy complexity, it seems to me that our desires are as mysterious as our dreams.

# East Village, 1984

A strange encounter yesterday. It's early evening and I'm in a respectable, well-lit gay bar with Peter. The atmosphere is relaxed, not at all cruisy, with most of those drinking seeming to be business people on their way home from work, much like a wine bar in London during happy hour. It's warm and I have on just a short sleeved t-shirt. As we talk, I become aware of a faint sensation on my right forearm which is partly behind me since I have my hand resting in the back pocket of my jeans where my money is. I'd been pick-pocketed a few nights before; my trousers were around my ankles at the time and the guy giving me head had simultaneously helped himself to the contents of my back pocket.

The place is quite crowded and as people move to and from the bar, they inevitably brush past each other. This is the plausible explanation for what I've just felt; it is like that

... like that, but different, and I sense the difference physically before realizing what it is consciously: the sensation I'm feeling is – can it be? – of a cock rubbing ever so gently against me. It is: the skin texture is unmistakable. Had this been six hours later in a back room, it would have been unremarkable, but here in this respectable daylight, main street bar full of city suits? I do nothing and the sensation continues. Definitely an *erect* cock, then. Intrigued, I turn slightly to my right, enough to register, without properly seeing, a tall person in a heavy greatcoat standing close to me. No doubt about it now: under the cover of that coat he's gently, very gently, caressing my forearm with his erect cock. I neither look at him, nor do I stop him. Surprise gives way to admiration: to be able to pull this off, so to speak, in a crowded bar without anyone but me realizing, is remarkable. Then a further thought occurs: am I even supposed to realize what is happening? The secrecy and daring of it is intriguing even if it's also (probably, maybe, but who knows for sure?) quite desperate. I carry on talking to Peter while very faintly reciprocating the caress with my arm – just enough to let him know that I know. And yes, I think I am supposed to know: within half a minute I feel a slight warm wetness, the sensation stops and whoever it is/was melts away in the crowd. I didn't see his face or anything else about him. I doubt I could even recognize the coat.

Partly on the strength of this I return to that bar several times and a couple of days later have another, very different encounter. Again it's early evening and a young man comes and stands near me, holding my gaze. When he speaks, in English, it confirms my sense that he isn't American, although I still can't place the accent. Nor can he place mine, asking if I'm French. I say no, English. He doesn't exactly freeze but becomes wary and very still, before saying, quietly, 'I am from Argentina'. The war between our two countries, over the Falklands, was two years ago. I don't know what to say. I don't have a quick line on that

war and certainly not a chat-up one; I disapproved both of
the Argentinian aggression and my own country's response
to it, especially the sinking of the *Belgrano*, but none of that
comes to mind at this moment. He moves away slightly as
if to go, but I put my hand on his arm and ask him to stay
and to let me buy him a drink. We find a table and talk,
awkwardly at first. His name is Lukas. He has a cousin who
was wounded in the war, but not seriously. He tells me that
the real tragedy was that many of the Argentinians who
fought were very young, poorly trained and didn't want to
be there or even know why they were there. He despises the
Argentinian regime and sees the war as a consequence of
its brutality and cynicism: the military junta hoped that a
successful invasion of the Falklands would divert attention
away from economic crisis at home and unify an increasingly divided country. He's politically astute in the way that
people living under oppressive regimes usually are – have
to be – unable to afford the complacency and ignorance of
we who take democracies for granted. The one good thing
to come out of the war was, he says, the downfall of the
old dictatorship. This I didn't know, although for his part
Lukas knew that the UK's victory in the war had, of course,
precisely the opposite result for the British government. I
sense he's too reserved to tell me what he really thinks of
my country's part in that war.

Looking at him I have this thought, as overwhelming as
it is politically incorrect: if those young Argentinians who
died were as beautiful as this boy I am even more against
the war. His smile: disarmingly beautiful. I'm not naïve
enough to think it's entirely spontaneous – we are after
all both gay men – but it doesn't matter because when he
smiles his eyes light up in perfect synchrony. It's also more
than the smile; his mouth is as expressive as his eyes. (I
realize as I write that there are people I know whose eyes
and smile are permanently, slightly out of sync, and that
these are people I mostly don't like.) We talk for a long
time. I mostly listen, watching the eyes and the mouth. He

tells me other things: I knew the regime was brutal and murderous, but hadn't realized just how many thousands of its opponents, again mostly young, it had killed and tortured in recent years. Eventually I take him back to Peter's place where we spend the night together. The love making is alternately tender and passionate and, at least on my part, infused with a kind of regard verging on remorse: nothing we do together can quite make me forget all he'd told me.

Still, after all these years, I recall my last view of Lukas. It was dawn and I was standing at the door to Peter's apartment, while he walked across, and then along the street. About 50 yards away, he turned and waved – no, more of a gesture of acknowledgement than a wave – pausing slightly as he did so, before disappearing.

I'll remember encounters like this one, probably until I die. So should it be a surprise that most sex, for all its intensity, is forgettable? The encounters I remember, some of which are related here, are memorable usually because they are also, I now realize, about something else apart from, beyond or even before the sex. In fact, to be worth writing about, for me they have to be. I'm not against writing about sex for its own sake – some of the best writing I know is just that – it's just not what I find myself wanting to do here. I'm memory gazing for sure, but it's a gaze which wants to be long-sighted rather than just voyeuristic. The same is true, more generally, of the intensely personal as it appears in this book: I'm not attracted to the confessional for its own sake; to be worth writing about the personal needs to have a meaning beyond me, or so it seems to me at the times when I want to write about it; occasionally, it's as if part of the intensity was always connected with this larger meaning, and, in that respect only, it's like a very faint reverberation of what might once have been a religious experience.

# Life and sex

My visits to the Saint, across several years in the early to mid-1980s, came vividly to mind again when I first read Moore's *A Matter of Life and Sex* sometime around 1992, when Penguin republished it, It had appeared a year earlier under the pseudonym Alec F. Moran and was published by a small press. I found it compelling, especially the way the picaresque narrative of a life lived on waves of promiscuity and drugs culminates in an episode on the upper floor of the Saint, where I'd sat with Peter, and at around the same time that we were going there. The most obvious thing about the episode in question is that the protagonist, Hugo, is raped there, along that same back wall. Did the rape really happen? Given that it's a novel, maybe that's the wrong question to ask. But it's a heavily autobiographical novel – Moore later described it as a thinly disguised memoir – and I think it's entirely likely that he was raped there, although I would have to say as well that in all my experience of gay haunts, the sex was always consensual. I've been in back rooms in both America and Australia where butch guys have come on to me very aggressively but as soon as they sensed my reluctance, they moved on. For all the S&M rituals, I've seen virtually no actual violence in gay male clubs. Friends used to the violence of some straight clubs were always surprised as the absence of bouncers in most gay ones. They were absent because they weren't needed.

As Moore describes how Hugo's drug-driven promiscuity escalates so relentlessly to that denouement in this place, the imagery used is at once visceral and cerebral. In one sense, it's regressively primeval: being explored by strange hands and mouths in an orgy along that back wall of the top floor is like being 'down among the roots of the forest ... amid the writhing tendrils that lived in and fed off slime'. But at the same time it's impossibly sophisticated, about how desire drives us to lust after impossible identifications: with 'the music wafting into his head and the drugs spilling into his brain', Hugo sees two other boy fucking nearby and wants to be everywhere at once, 'he wanted to be one of the boys, both of the boys and part of the forest of hands and mouths'. At the same time, he's aware of how the whole thing is driven by artifice, illusion and fantasy:

> This was better than the bathhouse. The dark was never dark enough in the bathhouse. Light played tricks, switching the pretty boy of one minute into a skeleton the next, the lissome youth suddenly chomping toothlessly on his dick, a body muscled and rippling in the spotlight that sagged and collapsed in the harsher light of the showers. Darkness was better. The truth was never revealed. Imagination ruled.

Except that imagination ceases to rule: someone forces another drug on him, probably chloroform, and he's fucked brutally before passing out and being found by a cleaner the following morning, 'bleeding from his arse ... his shirt covered and daubed in shit' and smelling 'like someone had maybe just pissed on him'.

It's honest, and harshly so. This is a novel which revels in relating, as truthfully as possible, what its author knows some readers will find shocking or disgusting but without the intention to shock. Moreover there's always something withheld as a way of getting the reader to focus the more intently on what's given. The scenario is familiar, at least to me: the hunt for extreme experience, life being intensely experienced only when one becomes reckless with one's own. When it first appeared a lot of people, including gay people, hated it. They couldn't accept an honesty radical enough to be, in its own way, ethical:

> For Hugo sex was both an addiction and an absurdity ... [He] ... could not regret anything that had happened to him ... because in every instance it had been his choice and in every instance he had been aware that he had no choice ...

Hugo never blamed himself for the way his life ended, and he never blamed anyone else either.

Moore could have written volumes on the mother-son relationship but instead concentrates it all in telling heartbreaking detail, like the way Hugo's mother remains at his bedside in the hospital minutes after he has died of HIV/AIDS, 'letting the fact sink in. But then she was worried he would get too cold, so she rang the bell'. Before finally leaving, she 'stared vary hard at Hugo's face, trying to remember every expression it had ever had'.

Moore died of HIV/AIDS in 1996, five years after the novel was published.

# New York and Brighton, 1992

The last time I spoke with Peter was when I phoned him from Newark airport sometime around 1992, on my way back into New York. We vaguely agreed to meet, both knowing we probably wouldn't, because by then there was an awkwardness between us. We'd slept together on a couple of occasions and Peter inferred from the fact that I didn't want to again – that these had been what he called 'mercy fucks'. Actually, at the time, I hadn't thought much about them at all apart from the fact that he and I didn't connect well sexually. That was crass of me. A couple of days after the encounter with Lukas, Peter and I had been drinking, smoking, talking into the late afternoon, watching the cockroaches emerge, and I'd been trying to convey what it was about the boy which had been so special. I tried to express my feelings about sensuality and why it wasn't quite the same as sexuality. Peter was sceptical and pressed me. I thought it was because he had sensed cant on my part, so I was on the defensive; I was wary of his intellect and didn't want to be cut by it. Also, he'd impressed me earlier with a beautiful, religiously wise

distinction between detachment and indifference; and what
was at stake here was something similar – a distinction that
made all the difference. However, I was serious about this,
still elated by the encounter with Lukas, and so I pressed on,
saying something like:

> 'Some gay men I've known try hard to be sensual but fail
> because they think it's the same as sexuality. It isn't and
> without sensuality sex becomes boring ... sensuality is an
> animal grace, an intuitive delicacy of touch, a heightened
> awareness of touch, communicating through touch ...
> separate libidos ... connect and equalize ... without
> merging. No, they don't merge – that's sentimentally untrue
> and would anyway be the end of sensuality – but there's a
> coming together which actually makes coming together less
> important, even coming at all.'

I remember thinking after I'd said this that it did sound a tad
pretentious, especially that bit about not coming, but, that
apart, it was something I truly felt then, and still do now,
although the euphoria of that time is long past. Anyhow,
expecting Peter to mock this, I was nevertheless determined
to hold fast. Instead, he changed the subject. It was only after,
when we slept together, that I realized Peter completely lacked
sensuality. In physical contact, he was wooden, uncoordinated,
clumsy. As he entered me, I had this feeling that in some
alienating way his body was a casualty of his intelligence
and that I was being fucked by an awkward loneliness. Later,
remembering what he'd said in the club those years before – *if
the truth hurts, you're probably living all wrong; your life is
probably a lie* – I came to think that if someone ever did get
to a place where the truth could never hurt them, they would
be either Christ-like and reconciled to their impending death
or merely human and already dead. I didn't knowingly hurt
Peter, but I did hurt him and, to this day, I feel remorseful that
I did. Ironically I hurt him because I respected him too much,
believing what he'd said about truth and hurt was true, at

least for him. Believing in his intelligence made me ignore his vulnerability, especially the vulnerability of his body.

So we didn't meet. A year or so later, I heard from a mutual acquaintance that Peter had befriended a young and delinquent heroin addict. More time passed and I had a rather formal letter from Peter saying that, as one of his former sexual partners, I needed to know he was HIV positive. A few years after that he was dead.

The bathhouse that Peter introduced me to was closed a year after I was last there. The Saint closed in 1988; later the building was demolished and the site turned into apartments. It would be nice to think that those who now live there sometimes, in the dead of night, hear the faint distant throb of disco, or a stifled groan, but I know they do not.

# Cruising

Why did we cruise? Others have asked me that, and I've asked it of myself, without finding any simple or single answer. Partly it was like other human activities: we did it because others were already doing it; we came upon a scene where something was already happening and just joined in. Even deviants conform. But of those gay men who I've wondered about, or who have actually shared their motives with me, the range of other reasons is wide and overlapping – from the happy hedonist whose thinking and feeling about the activity seems as genuinely casual as the sex itself, to the compulsively driven neurotic whose misery, far from being assuaged by the sex, is exacerbated by it.

For myself, I'm not sure. Certain things seem reasonably clear. Just occasionally I'd have an encounter which was almost perfect, which went from pleasure to something else, elation, and once experienced I was out to repeat it. Maybe most significant is that, as already described, throughout my life, right up to middle age, I experienced a low threshold of boredom. The feeling went deep, a constant though elusive sense that daily life lacked something indefinable but crucial; that security, even success, and especially professional success, was hollow; I would strive for success because at one level I wanted it, only to find that when it came it was dispiriting, like arriving at a long anticipated destination only to find it was no different to where one had come from, no different from all the places passed through to get there. Beckett said habit is the great deadener. It is, and so too is professional success. Thinking about it now, I realize this boredom was there as a child, too. Kids are said to love repetition, but I didn't. From a very early age I hated repetitive nursery songs like 'Ten Green Bottles Hanging on the Wall'. The prospect of hearing each of the ten verses, different only in the number of bottles left, was to me tedious to the point of depression, and to this day I can't listen to insistently repetitive music like Ravel's *Bolero*. But if boredom was one impetus for wanting to violate conventional sexual norms, it was all too easy to exchange that boredom for compulsion and vulnerability: addiction is too frequently the destiny of the bored. Also, I now realize that this experience of boredom was an aspect of the depression which has also marked most of my life, along with that ever present, but obscure sense of loss I've already alluded to.

It was also the source of my ambivalent attitude towards gay activism. In the late 1970s, when I was twenty-eight, I had an affair with someone who was nineteen. The age of consent for homosexuality at that time was still twenty-one, so the relationship was illegal. I remember once, when we were making love, feeling this is so completely right, so entirely beautiful, how could it be illegal? Later, reflecting on this, the ambivalence came to the fore. One part of me continued to think that for this relationship to be illegal is wrong; the law against it is the result of obscene discrimination and prejudice and has to be resisted in every way possible, including politically. However, another part of me thought: I don't care that that the law says it's wrong; actually I even want it to be illegal, because in a perverse kind of way that heightens the beauty and the rightness of what we're doing, of who we are. After all, I was attracted to the deviant and the dissident because it was so much more interesting – rarely boring – so why normalize it? When he came out to his parents and told them he was having an affair with me, they initially wanted to have me punished, if not prosecuted, then at least dismissed from my job. Then he fell out with them and left home and they left me alone. I'd been prepared to face their anger because ... well, because by then I was active in gay politics, but more so because of some simple, but perfect connections:

> holding him after sex as he murmurs, at intervals a child-like vulnerable, demanding, yet almost defenceless narcissism; only 'child-like' and 'almost' because by now, at nineteen, though legally too young for gay sex, he's enmeshed ineluctably in the anxious calculations of adulthood. Then during the day just watching him with no sexual intent and feeling soft surges of tenderness; at other times thinking I need to resist his energy: he wants to be an artist, intensely, nervously, urgently so. Remembering the morning he wakes at 6 a.m. talking animatedly of literature and life, at once spontaneous and performance. It takes an effort to show interest. It isn't just youthful exuberance – too anxious for that. I brush him off. He isn't annoyed, trusting me already with that hasty commitment that comes from complete self-absorption. This relationship is something less than love but still precious enough; I love being with him but I'm not in love. Less love for him than an attraction to his own narcissistic demand for love, an attraction which may be no less self-regarding than what demands it, which conspires with it, with the fact that we're all created selfish, vulnerable and demanding.

We weren't lovers for long, and after it ended he disappeared. Recently, I rediscovered a trace of his writing on an album sleeve. He'd found a record of Thomas Tallis's *Spem in Alium* at my place and played it over and over. I didn't mind because I liked it too, but I should have realized we weren't destined to last when he would interrupt our love making and leap out of bed to put it on yet again. 'Wait!' he cried on one occasion, without waiting for a reply, and anyway too late. Around the time he left for the last time, he jotted something on the record inner sleeve: 'Tallis. Religious art. Submission to power through beauty. "Where the submissive is possessed and penetrated by the radiant sublimity of the glorified"'. I think I assumed at the time it was a note for something he was writing, but when I came across it again recently (the record had become redundant, replaced with a cassette and then a CD), I only then noticed that part of what he'd written was in quote marks. If it is a quotation, I've not been able to locate the source.

As a teenager I'd had a friend, Tom, who also took risks out of apparent boredom, but he was different from me, full of life in a way that made me feel I lacked it. Boredom wasn't just about a lack of stimulus; it really did feel like a lack of life in me. If we did something stupid on our motorbikes and got away with it, he would laugh gleefully, ecstatically, and his glee felt to me like a spontaneous overflow of life. Whereas he would be whooping with joy, I'd be transfixed, savouring a slow-burn elation, like an addict who'd just injected, enjoying the high the more because, just for a while, it fed a yearning lack. Later, I'd try and answer that lack through reading, giving meaning to life through reading. Not a great idea really, because the meanings were all second hand, and often rationalizations of the lack.

Tom was probably the first boy I was conscious of being attracted to and the reason for that had something to do with this difference between us. In fact, I may have been in love with him in a soppy kind of way because after I was hospitalized, following my first motorcycle accident, and I saw the more severe injuries suffered by other bikers, and the jagged pain caused, both physical and mental, I always hoped that if one of us ended up similarly, it would be me rather than him.

There was something beautiful about Tom's exuberance and I couldn't bear to think of it or him mutilated. I needn't have worried: the girl he was seeing became pregnant, persuaded him to give up bikes in favour of a car and to marry her. They soon had a second child and moved away.

Cruising was also about adventure, especially as an adjunct of travelling. There was a time when, for me, as for many other gay men, the lure of a strange city lay in its semi-concealed gay cruising grounds rather than its official culture, although ironically, and conveniently, sometimes the most significant cultural landmark were also, by night and sometimes by day, cruising grounds. Museums, libraries and art galleries have always bored me in a visceral, claustrophobic kind of way; I feel them as spaces which ossify everything they contain, positioning artefacts within a cultural perspective as oppressively regulated as the temperature of their environment, and the voices of their curators. It wouldn't be long before I was heading for the basement toilets of these places, which sometimes afforded a more animating aesthetic encounter.

Cruising was also driven by curiosity. I've always been intrigued by the fact that, in the myth of the fall, Adam and Eve eat the forbidden fruit from the Tree of Knowledge. So their transgression was about two things (at least): forbidden desire and forbidden knowledge; pleasure inseparable from a dangerous curiosity. And there's something else about that myth: Adam and Eve were, we are told, in Milton's words, 'Know to know no more' and, of course, immediately wanted to know more. So you might even say that the transgression was created by the prohibition. That, for me anyway, has sometimes been true, even to the point of naivety: the proscribed has always exerted a fascination, while the prescribed has been predictably tedious. It was especially attractive when the two things were juxtaposed, like having sex in a library when one was supposed to be working, or when others were working. Joe Orton describes something similar in his *Diaries* – having sex with a group of men in a toilet beneath a London pavement: 'The little pissoir had become the scene of a frenzied homosexual saturnalia. No more than two feet away the citizens of Holloway moved about their ordinary business'. So, for sure, it was never just about the pleasure, it was about wanting to know the pleasure and everything that went with it, including the graffiti which was its evocative, trace expression.

An occasion when the curiosity about graffiti got in the way of the sex: it was on a beach somewhere, near a parking area where different people met: on summer days, holiday people; at night, most of the year through, gay men. It had that haunting atmosphere, at once harsh and sad, of public places with a quick human turnover. Here, on adjacent waste ground, on the exposed, still standing inner wall of a part-demolished building, just above where men had sex, was scrawled in black running paint: 'life is a race against the shadows'. I first saw it in the gloom of late evening, some way into an encounter with a man who was giving me a blow job. It instantly intrigued me, but what did it mean? Which or whose shadows? Was it about the futility of trying to outrun one's own shadow ... graffiti as a life-trace – a trace of a life which went badly? With such thoughts forming, my attention drifted away from the job in hand and I began to lose that certain firmness of purpose necessary for it. I only realized this when my partner paused in his efforts to look up inquiringly and perhaps a little indignantly.

Me: 'Oh ... Sorry ... I ... erm ... I was looking at the writing on that wall over there'. As he turned to look I blurted on, entirely from embarrassment, 'what do you think it means?'

He looked between me and the graffiti a few times before shaking his head slightly and backing away, silently and swiftly, into the gloom. The world of cruising was often comic like that and in the more interesting senses of the word too: absurdity and sorrow, hilarity and loneliness, gain and loss, beauty and banality were experienced as different at the time, and seem so still in this present (though to a lesser degree), but looking back are so close as to be all but indistinguishable.

My feelings of boredom were sometimes alleviated by encounters with the sordid which exerted their own kind of fascination, even wonderment. I recall somewhere around Times Square in New York, pushing open a toilet door and finding an exceedingly ugly man sitting on the toilet seat massaging the hugest cock I'd ever seen. Without the least desire to have him or it anywhere near me, I nevertheless stood transfixed. Maybe I should have been an anthropologist.

All of us who cruised were promiscuous, but to differing degrees. Some were ultra-promiscuous, by which I mean those who were on the scene at every opportunity and couldn't leave it without having sex, either with people there, or someone taken home, or gone home with; and once having had sex with this someone, couldn't wait to get them out of the house or to leave theirs. The ultra-promiscuous people I've known tended to be defended, damaged or both. The damaged ones were driven, maybe by some narcissistic wound, and while as seducers they often seemed supremely self-assured and socially skilled, were actually out of control for at least some of the time. They couldn't help themselves, and if you got to know them it became apparent they didn't much like themselves either. Those who were defended seemed more in control. In a way we are all defended in our sexuality because so vulnerable around it, even the most accomplished seducer. However, with them it was almost like a repetition compulsion: been here before, know it will probably disappoint, but have to do it anyway.

A boy called Colin was a memorable exception. Apparently, he was not defended, damaged or even bored. There was something happy-relaxed, even generous about his promiscuity. It was one of the things that made him attractive. Falling into his arms was comforting; like a hug from a friend you're really pleased to see. Actually it often started with a hug. Also, he'd never, but *never,* betray or denigrate people he slept with. In that he was in my experience unique: in a subculture partly held together by gossip and bitching, he never did either. I now find myself wondering if this was something of a calculated seduction strategy. After all, people who are most trusted are also, Iago-like, in a position to most exploit. No, that's unfair: Colin wasn't remotely Iago-like, and I never met anyone who felt exploited by him. Perhaps his greatest gift – and I think this was innate rather than calculatingly acquired – was that he was sexually protean: he could adapt himself effortlessly to the desires of his partners: whereas they might be obsessively fixed in their preferences, he was adaptable. So in a way his sexual persona was itself seductive, intriguing, even beautiful in a way.

'Casual' is the word we use to describe the sex of cruising, but it's the wrong word, as much for the mixture of intensity, anxiety and expectation that precedes it, as for the vague sense of disappointment, or joyful elation, which might follow it. Also cruising was repetitive, and repetition is another great deadener. There was a disco song of the early 1980s with a refrain that put it well: 'It can't be love [pause] but do it to me anyway.' My own promiscuity would sometimes become deadening, and just occasionally shocking. One night, falling into bed with yet someone else, who on this occasion happened to be a woman, I went through the motions, including reaching down for her cock. I was shocked, not so much by its absence, but because it felt as if I'd committed an archetypal sin of *confusion*, violated a primal taboo, one which reminded me of a dream – nightmare – I'd had not long before: I was having sex with a man, who I thought was a stranger but who, I realized at the moment when we both came, in unison, was my brother. The following day, lying outside in the sun idly watching some slowly changing cloud formations, it intrigued me to realize, or concede, that even the promiscuous have their inhibitions. There's real pleasure to be had in escaping some of them, or at least transgressing them, but even as some fall away, other more resilient ones remain, or take their place, making me wonder if desire is inconceivable without them. I also realized that I felt happier watching those clouds than during any of the hectic sex of the previous few months. No surprise really: frequent sex, the anticipated escape from boredom, was itself becoming tedious. Many have found this before, but it's something you have to learn for yourself, and even then – at least in my case – being reluctant to acknowledge it. Even so it was during that period of torpor resulting from indulgence that I first glimpsed, or thought I did, the lure of a chasteness where libido is sublimated into heightened consciousness and acute perception traded for stale pleasure. Well, possibly. At the time I thought: let me be chaste, but not yet.

Because this book is about a period when my sexual life was mainly with men, and because it was the callousness of gay promiscuity which blighted the encounter just mentioned, I don't want it to represent my relationships with women. If, thinking back on those relationships, I find it difficult to generalize, it's for obvious reasons: the differences of the women concerned, and the encounters. Having a relationship with a woman as a gay or bisexual man – that too made a difference. However, trying to sift those memories for something in common, has, more than once, brought this to fore: the perfect pleasure of being inside her, of always wanting to be more deeply so and of orgasm being a separation back into selfhood with no sense of regret or loss. Whereas in gay sex, he always remains distinct and separate, and my desire is inseparable from the difference which he is, a difference within sameness, in sex with her, I've sometimes felt the desire to merge and boundaries to blur. And whereas sometimes in gay sex, the intensity of the desire has been in excess of the pleasure it affords, I've rarely felt that with a woman.

Other memories which surface: the unanticipated new intensity of making love with her when also trying for a child (I later became a father of two) and the equally unexpected sensuality of her body when she was carrying a child. The incest taboo means the influence of the family on one's sexuality is at many removes and maybe only retrievable as myth, but just as in my homosexuality I imagine a sibling influence – searching for a lover who was also the brother I never had – so here I surmise a maternal one. And something else: being bisexual isn't just about crossing the gender divide in practice; it's also about doing so in fantasy. So, when making love with a man I've sometimes wanted to be a woman in relation to him. That's to say I would like to relate to him physically in a way I imagine – fantasize – only a woman can. Whether that too is the maternal influence I'm not sure. What I do know is that, for several reasons, it's a fantasy which, for me, could only be just that, a fantasy. I'd also add that in recent years it's become increasingly apparent that some gay men can love some women in ways, including sexual, that some straight men can't, won't or just don't.

I mentioned earlier that initially promiscuity had seemed like an answer to the depression that haunted me. To begin with maybe it was, occasionally offering an elation, in a perfect connection, as unexpected as it was transitory. But just as the escape from boredom was becoming boring, so at a deeper level what I'd embraced as an escape from depression, started to pull me down. Again it's no surprise considering where I was sometimes ending up. Like waking one morning – probably more like early afternoon – in an apartment in New York and confronting what had led me there. I was lying on a makeshift bed on the floor, along with someone picked up at the very last minute the night before simply because I didn't want to go home alone, didn't want the party to stop ('rage, rage, against the dying of the night ...'). The bed was surrounded with the debris of excess: amyl bottles, ashtrays full to overflowing, skins both used and waiting to be, upturned glasses, spilt alcohol, cigarette packets, empty bottles, half empty bottles, sachets of something I'd probably used but didn't remember using. The sex had been hard going because we were both so wasted by the time we got round to it. And now we both reeked. It had been the kind of sex which Moore describes well and which I recalled on that floor:

> straining for the relief of an orgasm which, when it came, was only a spasm without the shudder, an anti-climax

that offered no feeling of relief. Just a small grey wave of depression.

In fact, a rather large wave of depression surged within me on that occasion, *but simultaneously hit me from outside*. I lay there, incapacitated by this overwhelming sense of futility seeping out of every detail of that brutally clear, squalid scene, spreading towards me, creeping into my headache and intensifying it, and then seeping backwards into the recent past and (so cruelly), not stopping there either. The guy next to me woke, coughed phlegmily from somewhere deep down in his chest and groped for cigarettes. This was about as far as I could get from the riff on sensuality that I'd given Peter a year earlier.

A light had been left on overnight in the kitchen which was adjacent, a fluorescent tube which buzzed relentlessly and flickered intermittently. But, bizarrely, what most held my attention was a flimsy shelf precariously attached to a wall in the room we were in. The wood was too thin, the two supporting brackets too far apart, so that the shelf was sagging badly in the middle under the weight of some books and other stuff heaped haphazardly on it, obviously some time ago, because now heavily layered with dust. And the right hand bracket was pulling away from the wall; one careless passing knock would probably bring it down. Absurdly, I had this strong need to *fix the shelf*, perhaps the vestige of some puritanical ancestry which believed that depravity might be redeemed in good works. But the guy next to me was himself a visitor, hence this mattress on the floor and I had no idea whose place it was or whether they had the tools. Probably they didn't and anyway, for the previous night's trick to start busying himself with practical chores around the place on the morning after, rather than leaving as quickly and discreetly as possible, would be an alarming violation of cruising propriety and likely to be wildly misconstrued.

There are times I've found the sordid cathartic, even invigorating, though disinclined to find out, or admit, quite why;

desire transmuting the sordid into something else, something more. This occasion wasn't one of those times. I imagine that for most people, or at least some, it's on occasions like these that some instinct of self-preservation kicks in and they clean up themselves and their act. For me it didn't.

And a terrible irony: there was a period when, although it had already arrived, we didn't yet know about HIV/AIDS – or rather know enough. So in those orgasms – the mindless, the forced, the perfunctory and the depressed, but also the ecstatic ones – we were risking painful, messy illness and death; some of us were becoming infected, and infecting each other. We were culpable. Looking back, it seems to me that even the most hedonistic and predatory among us were also terribly and ignorantly vulnerable, if only because of our mortality and all which that implies, and so little of which we grasped at the time. It wasn't just ignorance, though God knows there was enough of that in those early days, because eventually we did know about HIV/AIDS, and still occasionally remained reckless and thoughtless and in denial. Judge that as you will, it made us more, not less, vulnerable, though still also nakedly culpable. At once vulnerable and culpable, an aspect of that uniquely human capacity to both experience and inflict suffering, inflicting it even though, but also because, we experience it. In this dialectic between culpability and vulnerability love may be the outcome without necessarily being the answer, and maybe even having something to answer for: when we love we seek to alleviate the vulnerability of the loved one, often thereby empowering them to hurt the more. And if it's beauty we're in love with, well, we forgive that almost everything.

Why did we risk so much in the pursuit of what was more often than not, forgettable sex? If cruising was partly about trying to feel more alive, that was not the same as feeling pleasure. If it was just about the pursuit of pleasure, then the realization, quickly learned, that more encounters than not would disappoint, would probably have led me to look elsewhere. Some gay friends into cruising aimed to fuck a pick up once and once only, quickly moving onto the next, until they could proudly lament that they'd been with every guy in town worth having, and quite a few who weren't. For me though, first-time sex with a complete stranger was rarely if ever as good as repeat sex with someone returned to, for the simple and obvious reason that you got to know them, or at least their sexuality, that bit better. There were some significant exceptions, some ecstatic encounters that kept me looking for the same again, but mostly first-time sex either told me I didn't want to do it with that person again – didn't want to know them better – or that if I did want to, next time would probably be even better. The legal notion of first-time intercourse as the consummation of a relationship is wrong in so many ways given that real consummation – the precious connection, sexual and otherwise, and sometimes remembered for life – usually comes later. The best sex I ever had was with my long-term gay partner, Alan, and this is precisely the place to say I cannot now understand why he ever tolerated me. Had I been him, I wouldn't have. Alan was to me the older brother my actual older brothers never were and, although he was only seven years older than me, he was also the father my own father never was.

Finally, I freely admit that I lived a strange and deep contradiction around cruising, one which remains inexplicable to me to this day. For someone as haunted by loss as I am, these ephemeral and transient encounters should have been the very last thing I went in search of.

# 5

# 'Death is in my sight today', 1990–1

On my way to kill myself one hot day in July, I stop at a garage to fill up with the petrol necessary to see the job through, and become aware of an old woman with heavy shopping bags trying to cross the road. She's staggering and in danger of falling in front of the fast moving traffic. I offer help. She asks me to call a taxi to take her home. There's no phone so I take her myself. It means postponing the act; I'm both relieved and disappointed: the relief is in the diversion: it dulls the pain slightly, the disappointment in the prolonging of the same.

With difficulty I get her into the car. She puts the hose pipe on her lap. Half a mile up the road she says: 'the shops were so crowded, but then there's only four days to go. Still, I've got all my shopping done now'.

'Four days to go to what?' I ask.

'Christmas', she replies. As I drive I could feel her scrutinizing me suspiciously: 'I hope you're not on drugs young man'.

I ask her again where she lives. She directs me, with great confidence, into a cul-de-sac, only to declare that this obviously isn't where she lives. We try again, with a similar result. Impatiently and desperately, I tell her I can't take her home if she can't tell me where she lives. I feel that the terrible resolve I'd screwed up for the attempt is dissipating. She replies with equal impatience: 'Are you a complete stranger to this area?'

'Yes', I whisper, now wishing I'd left her be. Without a moment's pause she comes back with: 'Well you can't be a complete stranger, because you're here now', and laughs joyously at her own wit. After a while we happen on the road where she lives. By this time, she has come to assume I am the taxi driver and offers me a £10 note which I have to decline several times. Realizing I'm not going to take it, she said brightly, 'Oh well, never mind, I'll see you again.'

See me again? I resume my journey wondering if she'd been sent to save me. Providence? I wait for the Damascene moment, in vain. Clutching at straws. If anything my resolve to kill myself is slightly greater for having met her, on the grounds I'd rather die than end up like that. Still, I had wanted to help her, so I suppose something like sympathy is still alive in me. Was it depression that generated the sympathy? And if so, might I snatch something positive from being depressed? Or is that clutching at more straws?

The first thing that has to be said is that such questions only arises if you survive severe depression, and some don't. They kill themselves. Despite appearances to the contrary, suicidal depression isn't the same as masochism, which is often a strategy of miserable survival, with the masochist proving astonishingly resilient despite or perhaps because of their misery.

During depression, I've certainly had a keener sense of the misery of others. I would wake to wish I hadn't, and often weep when hearing the morning news. The news didn't have to be exceptional for that to happen; the average litany of worldwide misery, violence and conflict would do it, confirming my sense that the essential uniqueness of human beings is their capacity to experience, and inflict, great suffering. Sure, the news was, by definition, exceptional, but then again it was by no means the absence of suffering that made something non-newsworthy. Depression opens you to the 'fucked up suffering of the world' which in turn leads to the desire to 'magically disappear' so movingly expressed in the final moments of the film *Mysterious Skin*. Later, having 'recovered' from depression I respond differently to the news; like most other 'healthy' people, I absorb it as background information while eating breakfast, driving to work, or performing any number of those simple chores that hitherto defeated me. With such pressingly trivial tasks to complete, I am likely to leave elderly people to the perils of the traffic. I don't want to sentimentalize the sympathy and empathy born of depression; it's subordinate to a powerful overflow of self-pity: in weeping for others I'm weeping for myself, and it occurs most acutely when I'm least capable of helping anyone. It could also be not so much empathy, but a painfully extended range of perception, a pathological sensitivity *to* pain born *of* pain, like the sensitivity to light you get with a migraine. So maybe it doesn't add up to much. But still: depression can sensitize you to suffering beyond your own, and sometimes so much so that the whole world seems to be in pain.

Conversely, there's a kind of myopia, an essential selfishness, in mental health. This isn't necessarily a matter of intentional callousness, although it does take that form, so much as the inevitably narrowed focus of normal life, of just getting on with the task in hand. I like W. H. Auden's take on this in 'Musee des Beaux Arts':

> About suffering they were never wrong,
> The old Masters: how well they understood
> Its human position: how it takes place
> While someone else is eating or opening a window or just
>     walking dully along; ...
> In Breughel's Icarus, for instance: how everything turns
>     away
> Quite leisurely from the disaster; the ploughman may
> Have heard the splash, the forsaken cry,
> But for him it was not an important failure; the sun shone

As it had to on the white legs disappearing into the green
Water, and the expensive delicate ship that must have seen
Something amazing, a boy falling out of the sky,
Had somewhere to get to and sailed calmly on.

Psychic normality possesses its own pathology, as when it
entails a defensive blindness consequent upon our being
unable or unwilling to bear very much reality. Sanity and
psychic health may be among our more effective – and
necessary – defences against the real. More commonly, they
just help us coexist with the extreme misery of others in the
world, so long as they are not too close. Psychic health is
increasingly related to the facile idea of 'closure'. Depression
refuses or reverses closure, in its own cruelly destructive way
showing closure for what it is, namely socially sanctioned
repression. Or is that the depression talking? Certainly, in
the early stages of depression, this world of normal human
activity seems to involve a desirable mindlessness which I'd
like to recover for myself. As the depression deepens such
activity comes to seem frenetic and foreign, in the way that a
speeded up film of human activity can make it seem suddenly
alien, and I watch on helplessly because everything that might
include me in this activity has failed: energy, purpose, resolve,
stamina, confidence. Oblivion becomes desirable.

## Sussex Campus, c. 1991

Later today, I'm teaching James Baldwin's novel *Giovanni's
Room* and re-reading it in my office, a passage suddenly
affects me so strongly it hurts. The protagonist David,
having just left Giovanni, stands on a Paris street 'in a faint
patch of the morning sun' and finds in his wallet: addresses,
telephone numbers, memos of various rendezvous made
and kept – or perhaps not kept – people met and remembered, or perhaps not remembered, hopes probably not

fulfilled: certainly not fulfilled, or I would not have been standing on that street corner.

It makes me remember. It was around 1979 and I was going to Paris, fleeing the affair with P which had ended badly. An acquaintance on the gay scene in Brighton suggested that while there I should get in touch with a someone called Mark, which I did. We cruised the clubs and one back room and then spent the night together. I noticed he had terrible scars around his ankles. It was the consequence of a suicide attempt, one of several in a long history of severe depression. He'd lain unconscious for a long while with his legs crossed and the scars were where the blood had stopped circulating. We talked into the dawn. He had a distance on himself, very fatalistic, but also wise. We got close, in the way that sometimes happens when people linger after casual sex and which has nothing to do with the sex. At the metro we agreed we should stay in touch. He wrote down his number on a scrap of paper and gave it to me. I said I'd call again before leaving Paris. I didn't. I remember clearing out my wallet a while later, back in Brighton, and finding this number. It took me a while to remember whose it was, and when I did I decided I'd call him, but again didn't, thinking I'd wait until back in Paris. Again, I didn't. About a year later, running into the man who had introduced us, I asked after Mark. He was surprised I hadn't heard: Mark had taken a massive overdose and then jumping from a high rise block he'd killed himself twice over. Could I have done anything by staying in touch? I don't know, but I should have called. *I should have called* and I feel, now, so abjectly remorseful for not having done so. I didn't call because at the time I was 'healthy', and with so much to get on with; I'm crying for him now because I know I'm heading for a low. Depression regresses me. When 'healthy', daily life accumulates behind me, becoming a temporal wadding insulating me from the past, helping me forget. Depression rips and blasts all that away, and helplessly I'm back with the lost and the dead.

Why does a book about desire and memory include these reflections upon depression? For several reasons, including because, in my case, I think depression has been a sickness of desire inseparable from memory, and where memory, too, is potentially a kind of sickness; of desire turned destructively back on itself in a way which is so painful as to generate a new desire for oblivion, perhaps through self-annihilation.

# The soulful illness

Because it's so hard to understand depression, never mind explain it, even to oneself, I went in search of the explanation of others, immersing myself in the burgeoning literature on the subject as well as entering therapy. Of necessity the register of what follows changes with the different aspects of that search.

The first thing I was struck by is the way some writers on the subject give an almost spiritual dimension to the experience. So, while on the one hand, the medical profession treats depressives as suffering from an illness treatable by medication, no different in principle from say asthma or a heart condition, on the other the experience of depression has become the stimulus for self-scrutiny and social critique, somewhat in the tradition of Renaissance melancholy. There's a dark-night-of-the-soul dimension to it – the sense that if we can survive it, spiritual gain will follow.

In the second-half of the last century, philosophical movements like existentialism and libertarian ones celebrating sexual freedom, tended to be trenchantly anti-religious, although, in retrospect, we see how they inherited tendencies which were quasi-religious, most notably the quest for truth-in-selfhood: existential bad faith and sexual hypocrisy became different refusals of an authenticity which, though painful, had the potential to redeem the self and society. Reading the growing number of books on depression, of which Andrew Solomon's *The Noonday Demon,* is still one of the best, I found myself wondering if depression is becoming the latest focus for this persistent, Western quasi-religious quest for authentic being – as persistently elusive as it is ardently desired. In depression, says Solomon, 'I learned ... the full extent of my soul.' Depression is becoming the condition in which those aspects of contemporary life which thwart the secular soul are felt most acutely.

It's a world view presupposing both an experience of the illness sufficiently severe to be life-threatening and life-changing, and a remission sufficiently prolonged to enable a reflective, exploratory writing about it which is at heart philosophical and ethical; and which believes that there is much more to depression than illness. Again, there are religious echoes here – but only echoes: the soul in question is, after all, fragile, ever in danger of being thwarted to the point of destruction, or rather self-destruction. Moreover, there's no possibility of conversion because there's nothing to convert to, only something to escape from, and for most the escape is never permanent. Relapse is likely, remission the best to be hoped for. The majority of people who have experienced depression once do so again.

It remains a common belief among those who endure it that there is some meaningful connection between depression and the better things about us and our lives. Kay Jamison, in her account of her own manic depression (*An Unquiet Mind: A Memoir of Moods and Madness*), relates how she resisted drug treatment because she knew that during her mild highs she was most intensely, most lovingly alive. In order not to lose that she was prepared to endure manic highs and terrible lows which were truly life-threatening. Others, too, find a positive outcome from depression but, in keeping with our times, this tends to be personalized and emotional, a gain in the quality of life rather than something known about it. Assuming one survives serious depression, it's true enough one can learn from it; horizons are broadened. Yet the same is potentially true of any acute or prolonged illness or any extreme or even unusual human experience, especially one which confronts us with the prospect of death – our own or of those we love.

And then there's the persistently fascinating connection between depression and artistic creativity. In recent times, the idea has been explored by, among others, Julia Kristeva (*Black Sun: Depression and Melancholia*) and Kay Redfield Jamison (*Touched With Fire*). Melancholy thinkers of the Renaissance thought they were treading a painful path to metaphysical insight. Artists wrote of signing Faustian pacts with suffering in order to drive their art to daemonic heights. Today the religious and romantic echoes remain, but the eventual gain of depression is more to do with a feeling of inner well-being. And if this resembles rather closely that state of well-being which, if the weekend newspaper supplements are to be believed, we can get with rather less pain through gardening, we might do well to remember those earlier times, and to be reminded by them of the obvious but significant fact that so much religion, philosophy and art has been pressured by the experience of suffering.

This we know: the work of many artists and some philosophers expresses the view that to be human is to experience deep alienation from the world. There is a profound dialectic between suffering and intellectual and artistic production, but this is a broad spectrum of suffering and not just depression. It makes little sense to reclassify such suffering as always involving depression. Solomon describes the 'acute awareness of transience and limitation' as a 'mild depression'. Which means that not only Shakespeare, but most other writers in the Western tradition were depressed, not to mention the likes of Joni Mitchell and Bruce Springsteen.

What seems to be happening now is that a new subjectivity is being forged from the experience of depression. It goes along with a sense that to be depressed in, and by, the contemporary world, implies a certain spiritual sensitivity. The depressed are seen as especially vulnerable to the crazy pace and technological chaos of present life, the consequent alienation of people from one another, and the breakdown of traditional belief and family structures. A century ago, Freud was citing contemporary 'nerve specialists' on how the ills of late nineteenth-century modernity were exacerbating the incidence of 'modern nervous illness' to a dangerous degree. W. Erb, for example, attributed such illness to 'the immense extension of communications ... that encircle the world ... All is hurry and agitation'. This was 1893 and he's not talking about the Internet, only the telephone and the telegraph. Freud, on the other hand, somewhat momentously saw the main cause of such illness as the high degree of sexual repression in modern civilization.

The problem is compounded by the tendency to collapse all kinds of human misery into depression. A century ago many symptoms now allied with depression would have been attributed to hysteria or neuraesthenia and more recently to panic attacks and/or one or more types of phobia. The sheer diversity of causes and symptoms now harnessed to depression is bewildering: loss is a classic cause, most obviously bereavement, but also things like loss of job and self-esteem. But then something like the exact opposite of loss can also be its cause: having a baby, getting a promotion, a new job, the achievement of something long worked for. Likewise, with the symptoms: in some people depression causes loss of appetite and/or loss of libido and/or insomnia; in others, compensatory over-eating and/or heightened libidinal activity and/or sleeping excessively. For some, depression can come suddenly and seemingly from nowhere quite late in life; for others it's an intensification of a life-long melancholy. Can it really be the same 'illness' that's involved?

And can the sceptical even trust the statistics? Here's a sample of some of the more cautious, as presented by Solomon, as of c. 2001: Worldwide, depression is the leading cause of disability for persons over the age of five, and it claims more 'years' than war, cancer and AIDS combined. Manic depression is the second highest killer of young women, the third of young men. Half of those with manic depression will make a suicide attempt and one in five of those with major depression. Previous attempts at suicide are the strongest factor in predicting suicide. Untreated depression has a mortality rate of between 10 and 20 per cent. Nineteen million Americans suffer from severe depression; 28 million – one in ten – are on Prozac or its equivalent. Some scientists claim the rate of depression is doubling every twenty years. Realizing, too, that other diseases, from alcoholism to heart disease, mask the depression which causes them, it may be, says Solomon, that depression is 'the biggest killer on earth'.

We should at least be sceptical about depression as the new catch-all for human misery. Those who are beholden to the philosopher Michel Foucault might go further, detecting here something quite insidious: a new classification of illness which is about empowering the professionals who treat it as much if not more than alleviating the pain of those who suffer from it. It might also be pointed out that the classification tends to be self-fulfilling: we find ourselves ill according to the labels; hysteria and neurasthenia have mutated into depression. Anti-capitalists will additionally brood on the profits of the companies that provide the drugs which increasingly are used to treat depression, while conspiracy theorists may believe that the professionals and the drug companies work together.

# Hamlet

Distrust of the category doesn't alleviate the experience and historical relativism goes by the board when I watch or read Shakespeare's *Hamlet*. There, before my eyes, is a recognizable depressive and while his depression isn't perhaps the main reason why he's arguably the most famous individual in the whole of western literature, it's certainly a factor. After all, Hamlet's situation includes some of the classic precipitates of depression, and his behaviour some of its classic symptoms. Sudden bereavement (the death of his father) is compounded by a further loss, one so traumatic as to constitute a betrayal of both himself and his father: the indecently hasty remarriage of his mother. His trauma becomes vicious when Hamlet discovers she's married the very man who murdered his father. He behaves like a depressive too, with irrational, violent mood swings and ends up where severe depression takes most of its victims: contemplating suicide.

The real confirmation of Hamlet's depression isn't in the famous soliloquies, not even in the suicidal meditation on death as a consummation devoutly to be wished; rather it's when he says: 'How weary, stale, flat, and unprofitable / Seem to me all the uses of this world.' That's probably the most widely recognized early experience of depression's onset: an inability to take or find pleasure in anything which all too quickly leads to a state of severe incapacity in which the smallest task takes a huge effort of energy in a situation where one has none anyway. Having said that I'm once again compelled to qualify: some people are able to hide their depression and continue apparently to function effectively. The first anyone else knows about it is that they've killed themselves or tried to. Lewis Wolpert mentions a woman who told him 'how cheerful she could be with her son at the same time as she was composing in her mind, the suicide note she would leave him' (*Malignant Sadness*).

So maybe it's only this which links modern depressives to Hamlet: when the effort of just trying to survive becomes intolerable one's thoughts turn to suicide, and eventually perhaps, suicide is attempted. Whether the rest is silence depends on the outcome. Yet here's another difference: whereas Hamlet holds back from suicide because he's worried about what he might encounter in the hereafter, that's probably the last thing in the mind of today's seriously suicidal depressive; they are more likely to be worried about making a mess of the attempt. In the early stages of depression, suicidal thoughts are inseparable from concern about the effect taking your own life would have on relatives, partners and others close to you, and that concern is, for a while, acute enough to resolve you to stay alive. Your own suffering sensitizes you to the suffering you'd cause. However, as the depression worsens that concern slowly diminishes and eventually disappears altogether. It sounds callous but the experience isn't one of callousness; you may want to care still, but you just can't. Something has been severed. It is one of the darkest things about depression, the way it isolates you totally from the people you love.

# Causes, causes

After decades of recurrent depression, sometimes severe, I'm less sure now than ever why it comes to me. The psychiatrists who dispense me drugs know it's bio-chemical; friends who are followers of Freud know it's coming from my unconscious and assure me that prolonged psychoanalysis is the only answer; relatives who disapprove of my homosexuality are convinced that is the cause; a brother once suggested it was the dubious company I kept at university; an obese neighbour was sure it was a combination of bad diet and late nights; a chiropractor told me it is caused by insufficient fat in the diet; a neurotic American friend assured me that it is the lethal combination of drinking coffee and not jogging. For a while, I did stop drinking coffee. As for me, I'm the only one who still doesn't know, or rather knows only that there is something deeply mysterious about depression. For reasons one never fully understands, it begins with that inability to get pleasure from anything, followed by an inability to carry through even – or especially – the most mundane of tasks. From there on, as I've said, people's experience differs widely but many end up having thoughts of suicide, attempting it and sometimes succeeding. That final phase is the most mysterious of all: it's not so much that the life force has been extinguished; rather it seems to have been turned against itself. Tolstoy describes depression like this: 'The force that drew me away from life … was a force like that of my previous attachment to life, only in a contrary direction'. Or maybe it's that the will to live and the wish to die share the same obscure origins. I suspect Byron was saying something like this, as well as writing from his own depression when in *Don Juan*, he says 'life's strange principle will often lie / Deepest in those who long the most to die'.

The mystery of depression is there, too, in the way that it's an experience so agonizingly lonely and somehow beyond the reach of communication or even expression. It's unimaginable to those who haven't had it and often inexpressible for those who have. And those who have struggled for the right metaphor or analogy without ever feeling they've succeeded. Wolpert begins his study, *Malignant Sadness*, by telling us bluntly that the experience of depression was more terrible even than watching his wife die of cancer. If that is both a shocking and a brave admission, it's also an honest attempt to convey this pain beyond expression. I have a low tolerance for physical pain, yet there's no physical pain which I've so far experienced which I'd not prefer, every time, over that of depression.

This inability to describe what was literally threatening my life *from within* is something I repeatedly found when inside a depression, and even more so when I come out of it; it was as if, at the time of being depressed, I was blocked access to its cause, and then experienced a kind of amnesia about the experience when recovering. But there was a moment of clarity before one suicide attempt; in fact, it was the feeling which determined me to make it; it was, as I've said, as if my life energy, my desire, had turned back on itself. Already though that's misleading, at least if it implies a kind of narcissistic closed circle. It wasn't that, and nor was it simply about the frustration of desire. The thing about frustration is that it's amenable to rationalization and sublimation – amazingly so in a spiritual context where it can even lead to the extinguishing of desire. Maybe a machine analogy works better: a bearing, a linkage, a set of interconnected cogs are there to transmit energy with its minimal loss through friction. If they fail, for example by seizing, the friction increases massively; the energy is converted into friction, which, if extreme enough, causes the unit to literally self-destruct. Freudians would say that my libido had regressed into and was destroying my ego; it's another way of putting it, I suppose, but I marginally prefer the mechanical analogy. Freud sometimes used hydraulic metaphors to describe the workings of the libido, and has been criticized for doing so, but here I see his point. Energy which is blocked or 'dammed' instead of flowing, builds up a pressure eventually destructive of whatever is containing it. Maybe such metaphors are only of use in suggesting that the life force isn't something we possess or generate from within, but something which passes through us, and that suicidal depression results when the energy gets locked inside us, as self-destructive friction or pressure.

As I say, these are only metaphors, but for me, during this moment of insight, seemingly granted only when death was in prospect, it was as if depression involves not so much a failure of the life force as its inversion, a negative, regressive intensification of it, the seized linkage, the blocked conduit. That's one reason why the fatigue of depression is intolerable. It's not the fatigue which physical pain eventually gives way to, along with the promise of cessation of consciousness, but a fatigue which intensifies the pain and consciousness of it. Pushing the mechanical metaphor, perhaps too far, fatigue is the inability to function not because the unit is worn out but because it's seizing up. The greater the fatigue, the greater the pain, the more heightened the consciousness. Thus the desire for, the attraction of, oblivion.

This experience of desire turning back on itself occurred most acutely when my intense but inarticulate feelings of loss became overwhelming. I said earlier I thought my depression was a sickness of desire driven by memory. Despite having spent most of my life on anti-depressants – and seeing too many psychiatrists and therapists – I'm still not sure it's an illness at all, and mean 'sick' as in 'love-sickness' or Yeats' soul-heart, 'sick with desire / And fastened to a dying animal'. The conscious memories were connected with something deeper, as unreachable as it was destructive. What surfaced into consciousness, and then only obscurely, was a sense that there was no one in the present who could save me from the loneliness of loss. Then, more in dreams than consciousness, I would have this related, more specific, even more painful realization, that actually there *was* someone, or *had been* someone, somewhere, who might have saved me, but they too were now lost to me. I was experiencing an intense desire which it was impossible to realize – 'realize' both in the sense of fulfilling, and understanding. So it turned back on itself, seeking to destroy itself.

In that prolonged depression during 1990–1, the pain was such that I tried three times to kill myself. The first attempt was, in that trite but accurate phrase, a 'cry for help'. Though I overdosed, I didn't really want to die, and I certainly didn't want to do the killing. With the second, a few days later, I wanted to die but still didn't want to do the killing. With the third attempt, shortly after that, I wanted to die and was now prepared to do the killing. I went outside at night and washed down a huge overdose of Distalgesic pain killers with whisky. I recovered consciousness later, amid a lot of vomit.

I was too sick to try again and crawled back into the house. Depression is intolerable but coming back to consciousness after a failed suicide attempt, still vomiting, is also bad. At least now though the pain was being experienced physically to a degree and that was a kind of relief. I knew I couldn't survive the night on my own so I called a musician friend, David. He came over, took me up to bed and lay with me, fully dressed. We talked, and I asked him about the lovers in his life who had meant most to him; it turns out I had known them both, though only at a distance, and I also knew that they were both now dead. The first was an addict who'd been to prison for dealing, nearly taking David down with him, and who died of an overdose in New York. The second had only recently died of HIV/AIDS. David was matter of fact in remembering them, probably out of consideration for my fragile state. He'd told me some time previously that he was HIV positive – he'd needed to because we'd slept together a couple of times. I'd always been in awe of his resilience and that's probably why I called him that night. I experienced him as incredibly resilient now; it wasn't an act for my benefit – I was lying next to him as we talked and I would have known if it was. But also, as we lay there I experienced an overwhelming desire to have unprotected sex with him. If that needs explanation or apology, I'm unable to give either. I tried to, tentatively, and he resisted, gently. Instead, he somehow imparted some of that resilience to me, and looking back I think now that he helped save my life, more so than anyone else at that time.

> I heard today (June 2, 2007) that David has died. It's eighteen years since that night when he helped keep a suicidal depressive alive. He saved me that night and I gained even more from his example across later years, during which he'd carried on creating, while also struggling with HIV-related illness. I mourn him with gratitude, sorrow, and a deep sense of my own inadequacy.

# Psychiatrists, therapists and analysts

I was seeing a psychiatrist at the time and managed to get an unscheduled meeting with him. He told me he had a patient who'd overdosed on the same drug, Distalgesic, and lived, but only in a vegetable existence. Maybe he was trying to frighten me, in which case he succeeded: certainly my greatest fear was to botch the attempt and survive in a damaged state, so I threw the rest of the tablets away, just in case. Of the several psychiatrists I'd seen in my life, I felt somewhat beholden to this one, not least because he made no bones about why he was angry with any of his patients who actually succeeded in killing themselves: relative to his colleagues, he had the lowest patient suicide rate and this was a flag of professional success. It was, he told me, a record he wanted to keep and he would be really pissed with me if I compromised it. He also did a deal with me: he wouldn't section me if I promised not to try suicide again. I later learned from my GP that this wasn't quite the deal it seemed; unbeknown to me he had tried to section me only to find there were no available space. And he dosed me up with so many drugs I'd have been incapable anyway of harming myself. Still, I liked him more than the psychiatrist I'd seen privately, not long before. At the time I was uncomfortable about seeking private medical care, but did so because I was desperate. The only thing he did, apart from sending big bills, handwritten on elegant notepaper, was to put me on lithium, a fairly serious drug, which anyway didn't work.

Generally, psychiatrists, like that one, administer drugs, wait for them to work, or not. They may talk with the depressive as well, but theirs isn't the talking cure. They have a lot of power over the depressed patient, and, of those psychiatrists I've seen, I've not been persuaded that they exercise that power very intelligently, as distinct from professionally. My first encounter with one was when I was about twenty. I think she had aspirations to upgrade to therapist status because she kept wanting to know why I came to see her dressed in black leather. I told the truth as I knew it: it was because I rode a motorbike, my only way of getting to see her and having already had one serious accident, which left a lot of me on the tarmac, and put me in hospital for weeks, I was now inclined to be somewhat more cautious and wear protective clothing. Now, I'd have thought there were encouraging signs of psychic maturity in my caution, but she was convinced there was more to it. So eventually I took off the leathers in the hospital car-park, leaving them with the bike, presenting myself to her in some moderately colourful clothing. Although she didn't say so explicitly, I think she took this as a sign of progress, whereas I returned to my bike to find my leathers stolen. Years later a 'real' analyst told me he thought I treated life like a motorbike – 'something on which to roar off into the distance'. I quite liked that, while wondering about the films he'd been watching. Anyway, this

'real' analyst thought it inadvisable to begin therapy at that
stage, because there wasn't enough time before I was due
to travel abroad. He feared it might throw up something
distressing that there wouldn't be time to work through and
that I'd try again to kill myself. I was willing to take the risk
but he wouldn't budge. Maybe he was right, but I felt it was
timidity on his part rather than concern for me: presumably
suicide isn't good business for the analyst any more than the
psychiatrist. I've often felt that behind the analyst's mask of a
severe integrity is professional caution and self-serving. Also,
though analysts are usually more intellectual than therapists,
though not necessarily more intelligent, they tend not to be
nicer people. In fact, some of the most famous have been
notoriously unlikeable. But the biggest problem with analysts
or therapists is finding a good one, which means, in part,
one who is suitable for you. Those who have been fortunate
enough to do so invariably recommend therapy, and I respect
their experience and their advice.

I never did find that person and I know this was partly
because I chose wrongly. On one occasion, I was asked if I
wanted to see a male or a female therapist. This was a decision
that had to be made on the spur of the moment and, because
I'd been much closer to my mother than my father, I chose
a woman. It was a mistake, as perhaps was the assumption
implicit in the choice, namely that the therapist was a kind
of mother or father figure. Anyway, after a certain number of
sessions I came to feel that this woman just wasn't very good
when I found myself predicting what she was going to say. I
now know enough about the therapeutic encounter to realize
that I should have told her this, not least because it might
have been a defensive rationalization on my part. At the time
though I couldn't, no more than I could have told my mother
that I didn't think she was very intelligent. So the failure of the
therapy was probably down to me. Did I, incidentally, think
this about my mother? I don't think so, but that too was a
discussion we – the therapist and me – should have had.

Once, after I had given a talk about the death drive to a

group of practicing psychotherapists, one of them approached me and said: 'I'm not a literary critic, but a therapist. And what I want to say about your paper is this: I listened hard but I did not hear the pain'. Apparently this didn't need a response since he added, quickly, 'I listen for the pain because I've known the pain'. This made me feel sufficiently insecure to feebly protest that I too was not a literary critic. Later I mentioned this exchange to another 'real' analyst, pointing out that it had put me on the defensive, and I'd half-lied about not being a literary critic, because I half was, but didn't really want to be one. Now that, I thought, *must* be significant. He replied, only half facetiously I think, that it's OK to lie to a therapist so long as you never lie to an analyst. Well, I was beginning to lie to that woman therapist, at least through omission, and that didn't seem OK at all, so I left. Even when I did try to tell the truth it didn't go as well as it might. On one occasion, responding to her question about early sexual memories, I recounted an experience around the age of eleven at my secondary school. An ugly boy called Evans, significantly older than me, would get his gang to round up a younger boy who would then be taken to the corner of the playing field where Evans would lie on top of him and simulate sexual intercourse, with his gang watching. I assume Evans imagined this as simulated heterosexuality, with him as the man and the boy as the woman. I might be wrong, but I don't think he'd have been quite so proud of his gang watching had the fantasy been a gay one. Who knows though what was going on in his fourteen-year-old head. Anyhow, occasionally Evans selected me as the boy–woman, and after I'd told my therapist this she sat forward in her chair and said quietly, 'You must have been terrified'. I thought about it for a while, wondering if I had forgotten, or been repressing, some terror felt at the time, but nothing came back and eventually I answered as honestly as I could: 'Well I don't think I could have been because I used to get an erection.' I could sense she didn't believe me and when I ventured the thought that an eleven-year-old boy would have to be in possession of a very advanced fantasy life to simultaneously experience terror *and* sustain an erection, I sensed that too was the wrong thing to have said. I know now that Evans was harmless and I knew it then, too, and one thing I *did* learn in therapy was that there's just no way I'm tempted to rewrite the past to find trauma where there was none.

I used to sometimes yearn for someone at once younger brother and lover and one therapist suggested this was an incestuous, narcissistic yearning for lost youth. That sounds plausible to me, though I'd add in passing that narcissism can be more intricate than is usually recognized and that maybe this fantasy is also about the younger brother I never had, and/ or my wanting to be to him what my actual brothers never were to me.

Freud left us with some profound insights but also made it possible for disastrous errors of interpretation to be made in relation to the same. For this and other reasons I have more than once felt that the only trustworthy analyst would be one with the integrity and empathy of Jesus Christ. If, though, I ever found myself in the presence of such a person it definitely wouldn't be through psychoanalysis that I'd want to relate to him.

When my friend P, who now belongs to the Anglican Church, reads that last sentence he asks if I meant by it that I'd rather have sex with Christ than be analysed by him. It wasn't what I'd meant, but nevertheless leads to our speculating on what it would be like to have had sex with Christ. I think it would be disappointing on the grounds that only the fallen can have good sex; or conversely, and more interestingly, that if it turned out to be good, this meant Christ was fallen. After deciding we both preferred the idea of a fallen Christ, and not only because of its implications for the sex, there follows a silence in which we realize we are probably thinking the same thing. I broach it:

'Would you want to go top or bottom?'

'Have to be bottom,' he replied without hesitation,

'seems kind of sacrilegious to go top with Christ. Unnatural even.'

'Except they do say it's only the sacrilegious who truly know the value of the sacred.'

'Mmm … Even so …,' replied P, adding after another longish silence: 'Thing is though, the more I learn about him the more I reckon he was a bottom. The best people usually are.'

# Illusions

I said earlier that being healthy includes being defended against reality, while being depressed sometimes involves the stripping away of those defences. I believe this, but doubling back on myself yet again, I have to add that depression can encourage its own illusions. For instance, at different times I've wanted to believe my own depression to be biological, chemical or hereditary, because that way one can stop searching for the cause, stop trying different cures, and hand oneself over for treatment, as one might with any other illness. One of my symptoms is chronic fatigue, and doctors have often tested my blood for illnesses associated with that condition. I've been disappointed when they've found nothing, being more than willing to exchange depression for a 'physical' illness that was explicable and treatable, even a serious one. Probably my most sustaining illusion grew from my first devastating depression around the age of twenty, which led to a suicide attempt which I only just survived, and by a strange happenstance. In a car in a lay-by on a country road I took an overdose and cut my wrists. I still shudder at the memory of doing the cutting. It's often said than suicide is an expression of anger at the self, a form of violent self-hatred. It may be for some, but I've always felt this is a view which ignores the terrible conflict involved in suicide: one's entire conscious self might want to die, to be free of the pain, but it has to overcome a powerful biological drive of self-protection, not against death as such, but of the violence inflicted on the self by the self, a drive as instinctive as flinching in the face of a blow. I suspect that most suicides choose a violent death only because they don't have a painless alternative to hand, or can't think of one. It's difficult to kill oneself without pain or violence or the risk of failure. When a suicide occurs, people dwell on the distress which led to it, often assuming that the act itself, once decided upon, was straightforward. But it isn't, especially not for a young person.

Anyhow I did go through with it and was unconscious for hours. A man noticed the car in the early morning while on his way to work. Becoming uncharacteristically ill later in the day, he decided to go home. Seeing the car still there he became suspicious and rang the police. I was told afterwards the ambulance crew initially thought I was dead, and I nearly was. I'd lost a lot of blood and an hour or so more, I would have been. In the difficult years that followed, I came to believe that to have survived such a close brush with death, both then and in my various road accidents, meant it was my destiny to survive. Egotistic that may have been, and disenchanted with that illusion I soon became, but for a while it was a sustaining illusion and I don't regret it.

I find then, after many years of recurrent depression, and much reading about it, I don't have much that's positive to say about it. There is one thing though: on coming out of a depression, there's a stage I eventually reach where I become glad to be alive in the sense of being hyper-sensitive to the beauty of the quotidian moment; it's as if desire has turned outward again, and a pathological sensitivity has softened into something still heightened but insightful, not unlike the effect of narcotics. It doesn't last. I have no advice to impart to others who experience depression except to try and be around people who make you laugh more. I wince at the seeming triteness of this advice, but believe it. I don't know if I've got the better of my depression; probably not. As I've said, depression, like desire, is mysterious. If severe, it involves an extreme incapacity to function socially; an extreme, involuntary withdrawal, a severing of oneself from social being. Sometimes one doesn't come back and the severance ends in a suicidal separation from life itself. A story I covered in my early days as a newspaper reporter has always stayed with me. It was only given one paragraph on an inside page – what we called a 'filler'; had there not been a gap in the page when it was typeset we wouldn't have used it: the remains of a seventeen-year-old boy had been discovered in a sleeping bag in some woods. There were 'no suspicious circumstances': severely depressed, he had taken his own life. And crawled away to die.

# 6

# On loss

There have been times in my life when being alive, being sentient, has been so intensely inflected by feelings of loss that I've experienced desire itself as a kind of grieving. But loss of what? It's seems implausible, I know, but I've never been able to say.

When it came up in therapy, suggestions were made: is it a primal, unconscious grieving for my dead twin? Or my two sisters who died in infancy? Or an introjection of my mother's grief at their loss? Is it to do with the love never given to me by my father? Am I grieving for my own lost youth? It's the early hours and I float these thoughts into the darkness; nothing comes back. I lie awake; he sleeps.

If I dwell here on the subjective experience of this loss it's with humility more than self-regard: I don't want to falsely universalize my own experience, which at some level I am willing to regard as a morbid, especially since most of what follows was written down either side of a severe depressive period. On the other hand, if this strikes the reader as maudlin only, I've failed as a writer. It's true that some future alteration in the reader's experience might lead them to then understand, or at least empathize, but it's the task of the writer to enable them to do that without the necessity of having that experience.

I've wandered into a church on one of those dull days between two seasons, seemingly belonging to neither. There's a shaft of weak light coming through a missing pane in a stained glass window depicting the suffering Christ on the cross. I don't know if it's the lifeless interior of this church, or the indeterminate time of year, but I have a strong sense of time moving more vaguely, more vacantly than ever, like the motes of dust I can just see drifting slowly, aimlessly in that shaft of light, which falls in the aisle, to the side of me. Just now, outside, I found an eroded inscription on the grave of a child from long ago: grief carved into stone. 'Down their carved names the rain-drop ploughs' (Hardy). That this child was loved once should be a consolation, as should the fact that the grief was maybe alleviated over time, and certainly terminated in death. And yet it all seems to live on through me, like a disease; I feel like a carrier of loss.

On the path leading through the graveyard up to the church, is an old cement repair, and in it a footprint at once frozen and fleeting ... at the time blindly purposeful: someone going up to the church inadvertently steps in the cement before it's dry ... a permanent impression of the fleeting foot, the fleeting moment. Barring the vagaries of progress (renovation, demolition, new housing estate) it will out-survive whoever left it; probably already has. A semi-permanence which only heightens the sense of time passing, of something gone: whose footprint? When was it made? Did the person know they were leaving it? Like a photograph, it's a freezing of time which is more acutely a reminder of its passing. The photograph: the past made present as stasis, silence and absence; frozen animation, the shadow absorbed into what once cast it, felt but not seen; a new way of being hurt, visual memory as loss. The person who leaves the footprint unawares is less a prisoner of time the he or she who intentionally carves the declaration of eternal love on a tree, a wound which will heal over in time and be invisible by the time the tree falls.

Amid the torpor of Christmas, aimlessly watching the film of Prokofiev's *Romeo and Juliet* with Nureyev and Fonteyn, I recall the friend who introduced me to it, years before, and who has recently died. His death maps onto Nureyev's in ways which are commonplace but still overwhelming: that friend embarking on his own creative life, Nureyev, at the height of his, now both dead from the same disease. Perceptions of loss commonplace yet so draining; each new experience of it seems to be telling me something profound that I need to know but haven't yet grasped, while at the same time only confirming what I already know.

Psychoanalysis offers various explanations as to why consciousness is pervaded by loss, including separation from the breast, the enforced abandonment of an original 'polymorphous perversity', being pressured into the restricted and repressive world of gender difference and normalized sexuality; the loss of parents as the first incestuous love objects, the loss of oneself as a narcissistic ideal, and so on. For me the most intriguing idea of Freud's is that the ego is 'a precipitate of abandoned object cathexes and ... contains the history of those object choices' (*The Ego and the Id*). In other words, *you are what you've lost.* Yet these are only explanations if you accept the psychoanalytic theology as a whole, which I don't. They aren't explanations of the experience, so much as mythical expressions of it.

The irony of loss: the past which pained us at the time, once past, can leave us grieving for it. Also, when remembering the past we forget how anxiously incomplete we were at the time being remembered; we invest the past with a significance, a fullness, it didn't then possess. Is that why it pulls at us so relentlessly? I know it wasn't then as I recall it now, yet that knowledge doesn't diminish the intensity of the memory, the pull. So, remembering Andreas, I force myself to be honest and acknowledge that our encounter

back then was embarrassing for both of us, leaving me with
only an inadequate mild tenderness already being displaced
by thoughts of the morrow, and the hope he wouldn't be
staying over. A couple of years later, when I heard he had
been killed in an accident; I realized that I'd known him
not at all, yet couldn't stop thinking about him, perhaps for
that reason. I'm reminded now of a friend who told me this:
remembering his partner, Luke, who died of cancer while
still young, my friend suddenly thinks of him again, decom-
posing in his grave. This was enough to send him fearfully,
desperately into the arms of someone, anyone, even though
– no, actually, because – he never really loved Luke.

This melody I've known all my life: why does it hurt
every time I hear it? Does it signify something irrevocably
lost to the past, or a past in which there was already irrevo-
cable loss? Maybe both. Each time I hear it I'm torn between
wanting to silence it to avoid this *remote* pain, and leaving
it on to try and recall what is being mourned so obscurely.
Maybe it's so elusively disturbing because it connects
me with a past so distant it's beyond conscious recall; it
mediates between me and this past yet without allowing me
to recover it. So the event cannot be relived, cannot even be
remembered, yet survives obscurely in this tune. Presumably
the same can happen with objects? Is that why we try to
protect ourselves from the loss of the past by preserving bits
of it as relics, mementos? Or, if we care too much, through
repetition? Desire is nothing if not repetition.

Recalling a past intensity is poignant just because it's gone
forever, and only now held from oblivion by the memory,
personal or cultural. Personal memory lasts only as long as
the life itself, and usually less than that. Cultural memory
lasts longer but only because it's constantly being remade,
which means that when a culture remembers something it
too often knows nothing about it. And memory itself must
die, as Shelley wrote in his elegy on the death of John Keats,
'Adonais':

Alas! that all we loved of him should be,
But for our grief, as if it had not been,
And grief itself be mortal!

We look back at the past with nostalgia, and in the future people will look back at our own time with similar feelings. The sadness is that we can't experience the present as the future will see it; we have only a partial sense of the present and even that is permanently incomplete precisely because of the necessity of living it. Hence that strange limitation of consciousness in the present, a present which only reveals itself to us when it's past. Except that we can never experience the past, only long for it. The present can't be grasped and the past can't be recovered: This will be/this has been/this will have been.

My strongest earliest memories are of the distress of parting. I think that what affected me the most was the parting not the closeness of the friendship or relationship. Before the parting the friendship was ordinary, forgettable; the parting made it exceptional, memorable, and its loss helped make or limit what I subsequently became. So I suppose it's possible that sometimes loss is not traumatic because it's the loss of this or that – the specific, that which I cannot do without – it's traumatic because it is loss: the indispensable only becomes so when it is lost or is capable of being lost. It is often said, especially of relationships: we only fully realized what we had when it was lost, when it was too late. Yet supposing it was only the losing which made it truly wanted?

When I tried the hardest to reach back to the source of this inarticulate sense of loss I come up against a stillness coextensive with spatial emptiness and absence, a meta-stillness within loss but also extending beyond it. Loss merges with this stillness, like a river merging into the ocean. There is the noise of life and there is the silence when life is absent. There is also the deeper silence only to be intimated from within life, but removed from it. It's this

I'm trying to express: I sense it in the winds of March or in the stillness of a foggy November landscape; sometimes even in the stillness of the late morning in any season. Perhaps we can sense it at all only when it's imagined as encroaching on history – thus Tennyson: 'There where the long street roars, hath been / The stillness of the central sea'.

In its purest form this stillness is beyond history, opening onto the silence of cosmic space, Marvel's 'deserts of vast eternity,' the stillness of total oblivion, in relation to which, desire, individuation, and loss are an irrelevance. I imagine this silence, this stillness, to exist even at the heart of a burning sun. It is pure non-being, not the same as death because infinitely larger and purer than death, but death is what restores us to it. I can only dimly intuit this, perhaps only imagine it, because meaning, like sentience, dissolves and fades the closer it gets to non-being.

Tennyson eventually finds his way back via religious consolation, or claims to: 'Well roars the storm to those that hear / A deeper voice across the storm'. I have never heard the deeper voice, and don't expect to now. Actually, I believe it's a human fiction. Which means that for me Wallace Stevens, listening to the unique silence of the snow, hears truer than Tennyson,

For the listener, who listens in the snow,
And, nothing himself, beholds
Nothing that is not there and the nothing that is.

Stunning lines. Tennyson puts a philosophical/theological idea in poetic terms; Stevens sees more acutely, more truly, more deeply than both the philosopher and the theologian.

We live forwards towards death, but another kind of oblivion is also always drawing us backwards towards an original state of undifferentiation. The essence of individuation is division and separation; as individuals we are divided from the whole and from each other, and imprisoned in time.

As isolated individuals we crave unity, the purest form of which is in the undifferentiation of non-being, from which we have emerged and to which in time death restores us. As we live forwards to future death there is this underlying pull backwards, a regressive desire to return to the original state of timeless undifferentiation; when Philip Larkin says: 'Beneath it all, the desire for oblivion runs', it's less the desire for future death than the desire to regress to an original state of non-being. The 'all' is future directed, the 'oblivion' regressive, like a subterranean current moving in the opposite direction to the surface flow. Freud mythologizes that desire as the death drive and it's a modern myth which equals that of the Fall. When he says 'the aim of all life' is death he doesn't mean we run headlong to our ruin – though some of us do indeed do just that – but that we yearn to return, to regress, to the state of non-being. As life flickered in inanimate substance says Freud, it didn't leap with joy but on the contrary 'endeavoured to cancel itself out. In this way the first instinct came into being: the instinct to return to the inanimate state. It was still an easy matter at that time for a living substance to die' (*Beyond the Pleasure Principle*). Freud projects back into the origins of life the experience of sentience as one of tension, vulnerability and lack, an experience sufficiently painful for the sentient to prefer a return to a state of zero tension and oblivion. The primordial first desire is the death of desire itself.

# 7

# Sydney, Australia, 1988

Arrived in Sydney about 8 p.m. Staying with some good friends, Patricia and James, a couple who live on Oxford Street, right by the gay scene in that area. The three of us go out late to a gay club. Patricia is intrigued when a Swedish boy uses her as a go-between him and me, thinking she is my mother. (Now that would have been a liberation to remember – to be given away by one's mother, to a trick, in a gay bar.) He's pressing and flattering. With me pressing is usually enough; add flattery and I'm anyone's, and this more through insecurity than vanity, though I'm not sure they are always distinct in the cruising context. However, I can't take him back to my friends' place (they quite reasonably had asked me not to on the grounds of being vulnerable to theft); nor can he take me to his (staying with straight friends of the family). Once this difficulty becomes apparent, it takes him less than a minute before he's dropped me and is pressing and flattering someone else. I wander off, discovering two more rooms upstairs, one a disco, and both even more teeming than downstairs. There's a real high here, especially in the disco. Immediately I see someone in relation to whom cliché is humblingly unavoidable: I can't take my eyes off him – one of the most beautiful young men I've ever seen in my entire life.

Same-sex desire can be interestingly complicated by identification, by sometimes wanting to be the person

one is attracted to: 'I want you' morphs into 'I want to
be you'. Or: 'I want (to be) you'. Maybe in this there's an
underlying envy of the other's beauty. Anyway I'm sure
some of that is going on as I watch him. On the gay scene,
very beautiful people intimidate me; much as I might
want to, I'm incapable of approaching them. So nothing
would have happened had he not come to stand by me.
He lights a cigarette and I ask if I can have one. He thinks
for a while and replies, very slowly: 'I suppose so.' Added
to everything else, I'm now mesmerized by the voice. I
can still hear it but I can't mimic it, let alone describe it
adequately. Slightly mannered and very deliberate, too
sensuously languid for camp, yet not consciously distanced
from camp either. The strangest, most captivating thing
about it is that once he's said something in this voice, it
erases for me anything else that might have been said. I
don't feel that immediately, but notice enough of what
later gave that impression, not to forget anything he says.
It's familiar enough to find a voice attractive, but finding
a voice sexually arousing – I'm about to have sex with a
voice? Actually it's even more precisely hopeless than that:
what simultaneously disarms and pulls me towards him is
an accent, an intonation ...

He's been dancing and is soaked in sweat, his shirt
sticking to him like he's walked through a shower. He's
dark-skinned, has longish hair, is unshaven. I can't describe
his appearance further. I've made the effort only to get
word tied. I must say something about the eyes: very
dark, very alive, strikingly clear, but without being at all
inquisitive. We look at each other for long moments – not
the usual surreptitious glance, but just holding each other's
gaze. He's measuring me up and this makes me even more
insecure. I've been with gay men who can undress others at
fifty paces across a crowded, darkened room with no more
than a couple of swift glances, noticed by no one else, least
of all the person being watched. This is different. His is a
neutral, casually calculating stare. I try to hold it, without

commitment, but eventually break and ask him what he's thinking. He doesn't reply immediately, taking a long drag on his cigarette; then, in that flatly even voice: 'I want to fuck you.'

'Let's go' I reply, weakly.

Outside he buys a huge burger. I eat a little of it; he most. We take a taxi to his place. In the taxi, he eats it unselfconsciously, it seems to me, even when the meat and ancillaries ooze precariously from the bread. I say 'seems' because I've found unselfconsciousness to be one of the more artful erotic poses. I watch him. Eventually he returns the look and smiles. Then laughs.

We get to his place and go straight to the bedroom and undress. He asks politely if I mind if he puts a plastic sheet on the bed. I don't. He rolls a joint; we kiss and play a bit. He tells me he wants me to fuck him and I agree but add that I want to use a skin. Without replying he takes a handful from a draw. I can't quite recall how we get into wild sex. The signals aren't clear and that's where things start going wrong. It's clear though that he wants to be fucked hard, urging it and enjoying it. During this, I misread his fantasy and do something wrong. He becomes angry and I back off. He goes quiet and I decide to leave. He starts talking again, still annoyed, but more conciliatory, telling me to come back. We start kissing again and it became tender for a while. We started fucking again, hard and back into an S/M scene with him talking slave. I have no interest in hurting him. It's a fairly typical S/M routine: he's the M, the fantasy mainly his and he is in control. During all this, we break two skins and he senses it, both times. We also take enormous amounts of poppers. We come together, at last.

Afterwards, when I want to go to the bathroom for a piss, he's shocked at the idea that I'm prepared to go naked and makes me wear a dressing gown because there's a guy asleep on the floor of the room I have to pass through. On the way back, my dressing gown is open. He hurriedly ties it up so this other guy (who was still deeply asleep anyway) can't see me. Strange. Then he goes to the bathroom. When he returns, he puts on his underpants and lies down on the bed where I'm waiting. He closes his eyes, saying it's time for me to go. I get dressed, but not without a long and fruitless search for my underwear. As I leave the room, he says simply, without hostility, but total indifference, 'see you later,' while collecting the used and broken condoms.

Outside the air is humid and a soft rain is falling. I eventually find a taxi. Sitting in the back, with the car window open, listening to the sound of the wheels swishing on wet tarmac and thud-oscillating over bumps, I wonder why the suspension on taxis is so often knackered. Still, it gives a smooth ride. The young driver, glancing at me occasionally in his rear view mirror, eventually asks: 'A good night then?'

I think for a moment and reply amiably, 'no, not really.'

Him: 'Oh'. Pause. 'It's just that I couldn't help noticing you were smiling to yourself back there'.

I hadn't realized, but I do know why: something like a sense of relief, almost of freedom is coming over me, and this because I don't after all, or any longer, want to be the person I'd just been with. I don't even want to have sex with him again. I realize we never even exchanged names and it doesn't matter. Despite a headache from the poppers, I feel calm – different from the usual calm after sex, the calm of temporary respite; a bit deeper than that, to do with having been freed from a desire rather than just gratifying it. It's because of this feeling of freedom and not because of the sex that I'm writing about the encounter now. But how free exactly? The driver and I are both silent for a while until I say: 'Actually, maybe it was better than I realized.' He turns around briefly, smiling uncertainly. It's only then I notice how attractive are his eyes.

# Life, disease and condoms

It's a couple of nights later and I'm in a back room of a gay sex house in Sydney, with a guy on a mattress surrounded by condoms. It's part of the enlightened culture of the place: literally hundreds of them are strewn around, for free, in the fight against HIV infection. Somewhere nearby someone is playing the Clash's 'London's Burning' and I'm taken back to a weekend in Brighton the late 1970s.

It was a time when most people I knew had stopped using condoms altogether. I can't fully recall or explain why, but it obviously had a lot to do with our belief that the venereal diseases we knew about were now mostly easily treatable. Anyhow, some time back then, I found an old, unused pack of Durex in the pocket of an old jacket and, thinking that they would soon be completely obsolete, put them away in a draw: in years to come they would be an amusing memento of my youth. On this particular weekend, I'd let some strangers use my house while I was away. On my return, I found an apologetic note explaining that one of their party had been in dire need of condoms and had gone through the drawers, eventually finding the pack I'd put away. In exchange they'd left me a 45rpm record of 'London's Burning'. It was a more than fair exchange, not least because by then the condoms were already years past their use-by date. I assume that, in their urgency, this was something they'd failed to notice. There was little point in me telling them this since the horse had, so to speak, already bolted, and anyway I didn't know their names or where they lived – I'd simply left the house open for them to use at the request of one of them, via a mutual friend.

The assumption that condoms were past history was, of course, to prove utterly, naïvely wrong. Their use was soon to become a matter of life and death. Such naïvety seems, in retrospect, poignant; we're always so unprepared for the future, despite what the past teaches. Perhaps unavoidably so, if such unpreparedness is one of the things that helps us get through. Ignorance is rarely bliss but sometimes helps us survive. Just sufficient of the future is predictable enough to allow us to deceive ourselves as to the extent of how blindly we live in relation to it: life as comedy on the verge of tragedy, revealed by history as tragedy.

> I recall a night with someone, then casually met, now dead. Remembered now, that encounter is most remarkable, not for the intimacy, but rather because neither of us imagined that within a few years one of us would be dead. Disconcertingly, the loss of this casually known person haunts me as much as the loss of others who were closer, even though the time spent with him was really not that special. His and my unawareness of mortality, our ignorance of the future, was inseparable from our restless anticipation of the morrow in all its mundaneness, of the next encounter, and the next, including (for him) the fatal one, if it hadn't happened already.

I'd become part of the gay scene just pre-AIDS, and for that reason alone it was truly a different world. One night, I was lazing around in a gay bar with a largish group of friends. One of them announced casually how he'd had to visit the local clap (STD) clinic. While there, he'd been given cards to distribute to his sexual partners, so they could be checked out, too. So he gave a card to someone else present, who then realized that since he'd slept with another also there, he, too, should have a card – and within a minute we all had cards. Our way of dealing with the issue of STDs was as careless as the sex itself: we laughed at the erotic network revealed and which bound us all together. No one worried about the consequences of infection because, in the main, there were none to fear.

A while later, I took myself off to the clinic with my card. In those days you were identified solely by a number. I was seen by a genial doctor and we talked motorbikes. The following day, I was walking onto the university campus when a woman jogger approached me. She was a visiting/exchange student from the States and in one of my classes, and was as ostentatiously academically diligent, as she was overtly physically fit. She asked politely if I'd marked her essay yet. No, I said, but it would be the first thing I did when I got to my office and I was really looking forward to it. This was a lie several times over because I'd just remembered that I'd started reading it the day before in the STD clinic, while waiting to be seen. I got to my office but couldn't find the essay. Then I realized I must have left it in the clinic on the magazine table in the waiting room. I'd got bored with the essay and started to read the magazine I was using to rest on instead, to write the marginal notes. I tried to phone but they weren't set up to deal with this kind of query. So I returned to my motorbike, raced down to the clinic and found it, still inside the magazine. I gave it an 'A' grade – and not just from sheer relief.

The salient thing about this student was that she was incorrigibly sensible. When in a seminar, we'd been discussing Shelley's line, 'I fall upon the thorns of life! I bleed!,' she'd quipped, 'Well, he could have walked round them.' Now I thought that very witty indeed, and was well disposed towards her, until I read her essay and realized she meant it. Religiously inspired, she argued for the importance of moderation and judiciousness in all things as a way of reducing the suffering in the world. In their reckless pursuit of sensation, romantic poets like Shelley and Byron were, she said, 'their own worst enemies'. Thinking about it, I had to concede there were several senses in which she might be right. Closer to home, the very existence of the clap clinic and my presence in it, not to mention the life I was leading, also kind of made her point, and I didn't even have any poetry to show for it. So yes, definitely an A. I would like to know what became of this student.

I have always hated using condoms: they induce in me the erotic counterpart of claustrophobia. Even when HIV

infection became rife, and was known to be so, I'd forego
certain kinds of sex rather than wear one. On this particular
night in Sydney, it is like that. Like many others though,
I have also sometimes opted for unsafe sex, and in full
knowledge of the risk I was taking with my life and the lives
of others. I admired safe-sex campaigners, but realized from
the outset that their strategies sometimes – and maybe necessarily – disavowed certain uncomfortable truths about desire,
insisting, for instance, that ignorance was the main enemy.
Well, sometimes it was, but some of us also risked our health
and our lives knowingly, not ignorantly. I saw a safe-sex ad
in Australia which I thought was streets ahead of anything I'd
seen at home. It just read: 'Remember: you are most at risk
when lonely.'

# 'True Faith'

In Canberra, where I'm based, I make the effort to meet
some gay activists and visit a local gay disco which they
run. One night, I see there an interesting-looking boy,
interesting, partly because he's so apparently out of place.
He's awkward and dressed as if he's just come from work
on a farm. He appears to be on his own and, despite
being obviously nervous, seems to want to connect with
someone. Partly because everyone else is ignoring him,
but also because I'm genuinely intrigued, I hit on him.
His name is Lachlan. He lives in the country or 'Outback'
and doesn't come here very often. He asks me where I am
from and when I tell him he doesn't seem sure about where
England is in relation to Australia, but tells me, with some
pride, that he's once visited Perth. Then he says: 'Come
and say hi to my Dad.' My first thought is that this must
be a spectacular brush-off and mumble an excuse, but he
insists; 'He's only over there.' By now I'm apprehensive: the
person he's pointing to is probably in his forties and looks

the stereotype redneck. And he's glaring at us, just like I imagine a redneck might. I back away but Lachlan just smiles, saying, 'It's OK he's not my real Dad. He's sort of adopted me.' Far from making things OK, this makes them just as dangerous, or so it seems to me. What if Lachlan hasn't realized he's in a gay disco? Maybe he thinks it's just a very large bar? I haven't been in mainstream Australian bars, but imagine they, too, probably have mostly men in them. By now, Lachlan is pulling me across to meet 'Dad', whose name is, in fact, Rob, and who continues to stare at me. I try to smile. Thankfully, at last, he smiles back.

The conversation is initially awkward but I soon pick up on what's going on. Lachlan and Rob are a couple. They work outside of Canberra, on the land. I notice Rob's knuckles on his right hand are badly grazed and bruised and ask him if he'd had an accident at work; I hope this is the case but ask because I surmise it isn't, and I'm right. They both laugh and Rob says the only person who'd had an accident was the guy he'd sorted out two nights before, who'd made the serious mistake of trying to steal something from the back of a truck. The next thing I realize was that it's Lachlan's job to pick up others, with the intention of making up a threesome. What is so striking is that while Rob could have beaten me to a pulp without even exerting himself, every interaction he's had with me, at least from the moment we spoke, has been polite, even gentle. Within minutes I trust them both. So I let them know, sort of indirectly, that I'm not into threesomes, and Rob gets the point immediately: I don't fancy him. Which is certainly and completely true, though I feebly protest otherwise when he says so. He says this is OK, and that Lachlan and I should go off together, but first we should go back to his place for a drink. In truth, at this moment I'm not much attracted to Lachlan, either. But, as ever, I'm curious – though still apprehensive. What decides me is that at just that moment the disco plays the track that I've been living with since leaving England: New Order's 'True

Faith', with its beautiful refrain about seeing delight in the shade of the morning sun.

I don't have transport so we all three go in Rob's pick-up. It's redneck perfect: originally a straight six, but now with a V8 transplant, huge tires giving a ride height for serious off-roading, and some customizing. It doesn't have a rifle hung behind the seats but I imagine I can see the mountings for one. I sit between them on the bench seat. The cabin of the truck smells of engine oil. Also, faintly, of burnt plastic, as if there has been an electrical short, probably in the dashboard, because all the dial lights are out, making it even darker inside.

On any objective assessment it's crazy to drive off into the night with them; if it's a set up I know the consequences are likely to be bad; I could end up raped and dumped in a ditch somewhere or worse, if worse there be. But, as I say, I trust them, and want to know them better. Rob drives fast. He's a good driver, too. Lachlan asks me more about what I'm doing in Australia. I answer vaguely; it just doesn't seem relevant, and anyway I want to know more about them. I say how much I like their truck, upon which Rob reveals proudly that Lachlan had sourced the V8 engine, rebuilt it and installed it himself. Lachlan is almost embarrassed at the disclosure, certainly genuinely modest: I'm falling for him, and like it very much when he casually rests his hand on my thigh. Although they are both reticent, or rather don't waste words, between them they reveal that Lachlan comes from a difficult background, left home a few years before and Rob had taken him in. The Dad-son relationship was a kind of cover for their being gay, but it was also true that Rob has become Lachlan's surrogate parent.

Was it so stupid to have gone with them? Not if I was right in thinking Rob was similar to the guys I knew in my youth. As a teenager and biker I ran with some tough types without myself being tough. So far as I was concerned they never hurt or bullied me, although their humour at my expense would today definitely count as bullying, and occasionally they showed me kindness. What I'd discovered from the toughs of my youth was that if you submitted implicitly (both tacitly and completely) to their superior strength, they not only tended to leave you alone, but also looked out for you, and to do that they didn't even have to like you that much; they looked out for you because you were one of the group. It was important though, that you were not afraid of them. This wasn't because they would hurt you if you were; the old cliché about the beast that attacks if it smells your fear didn't remotely apply; fear in someone aligned with, and subordinate to, them (as distinct from a rival), was just uninteresting, embarrassing, annoying even: it made them appear bullies, and that's the last thing they were or wanted to be seen as. Although this was a different culture and a different continent, I'm reading Rob in the same way. If I'm right, and some such negotiation had happened back at the disco – nothing was said directly, but then it never is – I was safer now than I'd been before I met him.

Of course, if you're dealing with a psychopath none of this applies, none of it at all, and I thought about that, too, as we drove off into the darkness. Then I reminded myself of what I also knew to be true, namely that there are far fewer psychopaths among the tough guys than popular culture would have us believe. Up until now, I've never been queer-attacked. I think this is partly down to good luck, especially since I've sometimes deliberately frequented areas that I've been warned not to. I used to like the risk involved, though unlike some I never found it directly erotic, although it can have a similar effect as sex in making me feel more alive. I also liked the challenge of a potentially dangerous scenario. As we drove through the darkness I remembered one place I was warned not to go was in New York, at the end of Christopher Street, where it meets the waterfront. Of course, I went, and quite often, because curious. Beforehand though I always put most of my money in my shoe, just leaving about $20 in my wallet. On one occasion, as I got to the river, a young black man approached me. I paused, looked at him directly, smiled openly and spoke just enough to make sure he could hear I wasn't American. Maybe I was being reckless, but I wasn't afraid. I have no idea to this day if he was intending to mug me, or looking for a trick, paying or otherwise, or both, or was just out for a walk. All I know is that he fell into step with me and we walked together for maybe half a mile down towards Hudson Square talking on and off. He eventually told me he had no money and I said I'd give him what I could. I took out the $20 and gave him $15, saying I needed the $5 to get home. He said to keep $10, but I insisted the $5 would do. Then he suddenly split off and disappeared. Another time down there, I met a white boy who definitely was out for paying trade. He came on to me aggressively because he thought I was trespassing on his patch but when I made it clear I was just a visitor with a strange accent he became curious, then friendly, and he agreed to show me around later. His name was Dean and he took me to the Times Square area and some of the sleaziest sex haunts I've even encountered – small rooms with makeshift stages on which boys did perfunctory strip routines for much older men, most of whom were obese, chain-smoking and chain-drinking. He knew all the boys and introduced me to them as his 'buddy from London'. I hadn't said I was from London, only England, but it became clear the city had more kudos than the country, being somewhere some of them wanted to visit, having heard tricking was more lucrative there. Again, they were cautiously friendly, once it was apparent my presence was temporary. I got talking to one boy who said he was twenty-three but looked about seventeen, painfully thin with scar-like darkness around sunken eyes. I asked, indirectly, if he ever wanted to do something else. His replied that yes, his ambition was to get in with a richer set up town, as one friend had already: 'He has a regular John who's already bought him a Chevy. It ain't new but not far off, and most of the time the guy only wants vanilla stuff.'

That prompted me to ask if he ever wanted to leave the game altogether. He looked surprised at the question, then suspicious: 'Shit man, you one of them church freaks?!' (I later learn that sometimes religious types come into the clubs to try and 'rescue' them). I assured him I wasn't, but it took Dean, who'd overheard this, to vouch for me, speaking as if he'd known me for a lifetime rather than a couple of hours.

The journey to Rob's place takes about half an hour. I have no idea where or in which direction we are going. When we get there it's too dark to make out much, and when he turns the engine off and we get out of the car it's deeply silent. As usual, out of habit, I look up. The stars, oh the stars: for a moment I'm dissolved by the sight, realizing visually and with pleasure what I know otherwise: that, in relation to that vastness, I'm nothing, just a fleeting pinpoint of sentience. The residual tension in me disperses and I feel an equilibrium and the beginning of a slow-burn elation. I want nothing more than to be here, the more so for not knowing exactly where; nothing more than to be beneath this night sky, with these strangers. I follow them into the house, now afraid of nothing: I don't matter, and nor does it matter either that I don't know what's going to happen next.

Inside it's drab and makeshift, the lighting dim, forlorn. Rob gets out some dubious looking spirits. I ask if it's OK if we go out and drink on the porch. We do, with Rob switching off the lights so as not to attract insects. Sitting in the dark, we talk about the need they have to disguise their relationship, about their not considering themselves to be gay, but not having anything against most gays, apart maybe from the fact that they look down on the likes of them. Eventually Rob declares, probably diplomatically, that he's working the next day and has to get some sleep. He gives the keys of the truck to Lachlan, telling him to stay out, or over, for as long as he wants. It's bizarre: Lachlan and I drive away into the night with Bob on the porch waving us off, like a proud Dad seeing his son take off on a first date in the family car.

We return to Canberra, and for a while motor around areas Lachlan knows to be cruising grounds, but it's all quiet so we decide to go back to my place. He seems more self-confident now he's on his own and talks more, too. He really does see Rob as a father figure. He trusts him and I think that he loves him, though he doesn't use the word. I sense he's glad enough to have sex with Rob, but that it isn't the most important thing in their relationship. He won't talk about his own family, although he does tell me that he grew up by a river not far away and that sometime he will take me there swimming. Somehow we get onto the subject of lesbians, about whom, like some other gay men in Australia, he is contemptuous, calling them 'diesel-dikes'. I try to talk him around, on the grounds that there are lots of different kinds of lesbians, just as there were different kinds of gay men, he and I being pretty different, for instance, but he isn't persuaded – saying they are all aggressive imitations of men. There it is again, something I'd encountered before among gay men in this country: antagonism to lesbians as part of a deeper misogyny.

Physically Lachlan reminds me of another boy I'd known only slightly, and at a distance, but who I've never forgotten. He appeared on the club scene in Brighton in the early 1980s. The only thing I knew about him was that he came from one of the local sink estates. Like Lachlan, he was gay without any gay signifiers in his appearance or manner. I saw him many times in the clubs and was always struck by his beauty: lean, muscular, worn and tired features but with eyes very much still alive. He'd dance stripped to the waist and he was a good dancer too. Once I encountered him exiting a toilet cubicle in the club, where he'd just done a line; we hesitated for a split second, acknowledging each other, though awkwardly, because unprepared. That was the closest I got to him. He disap-peared for a while, then reappeared, and on this occasion he was sitting away from the bar, in a shadowed area, and crying. Weeping really – utterly, helplessly distraught, and being comforted by an older man who I could tell didn't know him well. It was just so unusual to see – in any club, but especially that one. That it was almost shocking was, well, shocking, given that crying shouldn't be so, especially in a place where some of the other things that happened there perhaps should have been, but weren't. That was the last time I saw him, and I've never forgotten him because on occasions like now he comes suddenly to mind and I'm left wondering yet again: *why was he crying so abjectly?*

Back at my place, Lachlan and I take a shower together. Like that other boy, he has a slight build but sculpted body – shoulders strong, but not too broad, thin waist, full arse. His isn't the blown muscle of the gym, just that of someone young who works hard physically. He's gracefully strong, moves lithely, sensitive to touch, and seemingly unaware of his beauty, even when naked. Something else I like is the way he undresses, or rather doesn't, just shrugging off his loose fitting clothes in seconds, leaving them where they lie. I find myself comparing it with another encounter with a much older man, whose age was a problem, but less so than the off-putting way he undressed, neatly folding his trousers, standing there in his shirt-tails and tie as he did so, then dealing with them similarly.

I'm not sure he is conscious of doing so, but when we are naked Lachlan becomes almost protective towards me, perhaps as Rob is towards him. I find this seductive and realize that I want him to fuck me. So I'm mildly disappointed when, in bed, he quickly offers himself to me. It seems more like a gesture of friendship than desire, with something almost routine about it, as if (I wonder) it's expected of him. Again, I feel that actually sex isn't that important to him, so I white-lie to the effect of not being much into fucking, and he seems happy with that, though again I can't be sure. He isn't much into kissing either, but that, for me, was non-negotiable, and I insist on showing him how. He takes to it. Tender was the night, or rather the dawn.

# Sydney Mardi Gras

This stay in Sydney has been arranged to coincide with the gay Mardi Gras. I've met a social worker called Peter who's offered to show me the scene. One night, he mysteriously, not to say suspiciously, appears with a car, with which we pick up a young man who, on the plus side is attractive, on the downside is dressed in a suit and tie and drunk. We are parked up in an area of sparse woodland, where exactly I've no idea, with Peter behind the wheel, me in the back with the young man. I'm about to kiss him tentatively when he suddenly blurts out, plaintively, 'Oh God ... I think I'm straight.' This strikes me as odd, then funny, then hilarious. Peter starts laughing, too, and soon we are helplessly creased up in the way that only dope can make you, each feeding off the other's hilarity. Then the boy says, 'I think I'm going to throw up'. Peter leans back from the front seat and deftly opens the rear door, whereupon I push the boy out and we drive off. After 100 yards or so, I tell Peter to stop the car. He protests but I insist, get out and go back to the boy. He's kneeling, wretching. I hate the stench of vomit even more than of shit, seeing in it too clearly the visceral ugliness of what allows the body to live. It's not the skull beneath the skin from which we recoil, not even flesh and blood, but shit, vomit and reeking entrails. So why does desire lead us so obsessively to and into the orifices which go there? Memory of a scene in a TV drama: a couple drunkenly French-kissing when one of them suddenly vomits over the other ... Desire and disgust, opposite yet inseparable, desire now overriding disgust, disgust or at least distaste now reclaiming ground as desire wanes ... I'm sorely tempted

to go, but wait until he'd finished then help him over to a
tree and sit him against it. Peter calls impatiently for me to
come back to the car and I call back telling him to go on
without me: I'll catch up with him later. He doesn't need
much encouragement and speeds off.

He's crying now, quietly, and mumbles something about
his head being messed up. I know from experience with
distressed students and friends – and, come to think of it,
myself too – that when someone's in this state of self-pity
the more you say the less they hear. If you're going to say
anything at all, bide your time, keep it brief and make it
count. So we sit there with him sniffling. I become aware of
the silence of the night, despite the sounds of the city, and
looking up can see the stars, though only faintly, and tell
him so. He doesn't reply or even look up; maybe he doesn't
even hear me. I try to think of something to say that might
make him laugh, but can't.

Eventually he speaks again: 'I don't know what I am.
Just don't know.'

So, now is probably the time to say something: 'Well,
so what? Being unsure of what or who you are might just
make your life more interesting. Less boring. And I for one
don't care what you are. Very few people do, or will. Your
parents might, but then they fuck you up, so their opinion
doesn't count.'

And with that I get up and leave, but not before tousling
his hair in a gesture which I judge – hope – to be as appro-
priate for a boy who likes boys, as for one who likes girls.
Or indeed one who likes both. I hope he ends up liking both.

So here I am again, alone and without bearings on a
warm night in a strange city, teeming with distracted life, a
significant part of it in search of pleasure. I follow the lights
and traffic and eventually come to an entrance to the Mardi
Gras disco. By now it's around 3 a.m. It's a huge event, full
of the promise of adventure, and I'm about to enter the fray
when there emerges from the entrance a youth with the
physique of Nureyev and dressed only a skimpiest of loin

cloths. We get talking. His name is Lindon, he's in a filthy mood and is going home. His boyfriend, an older man, has done something unforgivable: Lindon had made, especially for the Mardi Gras, a costume which included some angel wings. His boyfriend had torn the costume off, including the wings. We talk for a while and I suggest if he's going home I'll walk with him. On the way we deviate into a park and begin to have sex on a bench. Looking over Lindon's shoulder I suddenly notice an elderly couple with a small dog, all *three* watching us intently. I whisper their presence to Lindon who turns round and stares them out until they move on, although the dog keeps giving us long backward glances.

As I write this, I'm suddenly reminded of a wickedly funny episode in Moore's *A Matter of Life and Sex,* taking the picaresque to new heights; David, the protagonist, is having sex in a car with a stranger when an old lady walking her dog peers into the vehicle:

> She was transfixed. David smiled at her. She walked away and he watched her reflection in the wing mirror as he heaved a load of pent-up spunk into the driver's mouth. The driver had no idea what was happening. The lady was writing down the car's registration number ... while her poodle shat on the verge.

I lack Lindon's bravado and persuade him that we should leave the park. By now it's approaching dawn and the city's early-shift workers are on the move. It's all coldly removed from the hedonism of the Mardi Gras. These workers stare incredulously at this Adonis figure, all but naked, strolling confidently down the street. Some of them jeer and I begin to worry. Then Lindon reveals that in the band of his scanty loin cloth he has a cleverly concealed small knife. I can't imagine him using it, but then that night – actually my whole time in Australia – had been full of surprises. Eventually we come to our parting of ways and agree that he'll come to my place – actually Patricia and James's place – the following afternoon. I don't really expect him to turn up but he does, and we make love, smoke some dope, talk – he tells me something of his wonderfully delinquent life to date, and that he's still furious with his boyfriend, an anger of which I seem to be the main beneficiary – drink, make love some more and then he leaves.

# Circle of desire

It's later the same day, and I'm still feeling happy from the time with Lindon. I don't want more sex, but decide to go out anyway. I feel relaxed, and just want to watch the human comedy with no compulsion to participate. I choose the Midnight Shift – the one with the disco upstairs, where I met the boy whose name I never got. Typical irony: despite having had no desire to cruise, the first guy I speak to – he's on the door – offers to meet up at the end of his shift (3 a.m.). He's nice; not to be forgotten. I doubt now however (two days later) whether I could recognize him again. Him apart, I see no one I like – but then I'm not looking for anyone. There's one interesting guy with a very adolescent masculinity, especially in the way he holds himself – but I'm not looking for sex. I dance for a while and then wander out into the street for a while with the intention of going I don't know where. Somewhere up near Oxford Towers I'm vaguely aware of someone behind me. Moments later a boy appears at my elbow. I forget exactly how conversation starts but its drift is predictable. I say something which makes him laugh; his laugh is so engaging, and after a few moments infectious. I tell him I don't want sex. With that disarming directness which invariably melts me he asks: 'Have you done it already tonight?'

I thought he would not spend further time on someone who had, and, not wanting him to leave immediately, and also because I am being half-tempted, I tell him no. His name is Ken.

We go down to the Exchange for a drink. It's late and busy with that atmosphere that sometimes only lasts for 30 minutes at the height of the evening: lots of erotic energy and the illusion of everyone synchronizing with each other. I start flirting with him; whispering outrageous things we'd do tomorrow and biting his neck and ear. To me he's quite beautiful, despite, or because of, looking worn for his age – he is (he says) twenty – and being unwashed. And that laugh … for long moments, we seem perfectly connected in the give and take of flirtation, laughter and arousal. He has this neat trick of taking the ice from his drink into his mouth and then passing it into mine when kissing. In this corner, while around us other possible liaisons are being initiated, faltering, abandoned or confirmed, we're like kids: he undoes my flies and feels my cock while another older man smiles benevolently at us from nearby. Ken suggests we go to a rent room nearby. Six dollars each. We get to the room, up some narrow stairs somewhere opposite the Exchange – I try to find them again later but can't – but a guy at the desk says said they close in two minutes flat. We leave and start searching for a secluded doorway. Sometime earlier in this encounter we'd decided – no, Ken had decided, I remember his quiet firmness, but still laughing as he'd said it – that he wouldn't let me fuck him but that he was going to blow me. We find ourselves in someone's dilapidated yard, only a few square feet, right up against a window. Though apprehensive by now, I really want this and I'm hard already. And, as he starts to blow me I recall that right there in my pocket, I have a new bottle of amyl bought earlier. We both inhale deeply and there follows a moment of pure ecstasy. That yard: so perfectly stark and us so perfectly exposed … me outside of myself looking at myself with him, one of his hands flat against my stomach, one of mine in his hair. Suddenly he starts: he's seen movement at the window. It's OK, if we hear someone in the house we can run if necessary. But wait – arousal makes one careless (only love makes one truly reckless): if someone has phoned the law they could be on their way and we'd be trapped here: their way in is our only way out. Quickly we move back out on the street. There has to be another yard. We both want to recreate that moment. It proves difficult. Eventually we climb into another one, even smaller and more wrecked than the first. More amyl. Ken pulls back from me, and at the moment I look down he looks up; with my cock still in his mouth our eyes meet. Then it happens, suddenly and unexpectedly: an exhilarating connection in a fleeting glance, an irreverent communion, a perfect circle of narcissistic desire passing through and briefly connecting two strangers. Longing stilled. Orgasm, when it comes is just a culmination, a lesser intensity that what led to it. For the moment that connection makes everything else irrelevant, until the ordinariness of the surroundings seeps back into consciousness, and we rearrange our clothes, hurriedly make our way back to the road, and part.

# The entirely beautiful

Two days later I went looking in the Exchange for Ken. No sign. I saw one interesting boy, but it's soon apparent he's one of the cluey set, transiently visible in every gay club, youths who invest too much of their lives in the scene, recognizable by their prettiness rather than beauty, and their highly tuned fashion sense, always of the moment and rarely original. Their dance routines, now *de rigueur*, would have been regarded by them as gauche a year before, and a year on will be derided as too embarrassing for words. I've always been intrigued by these boys' passive demand for recognition, and the way they can instantly detect if they've attracted it, even from someone on the other side of a crowded dimly lit bar. Theirs is a permanently insecure narcissism measuring worth in terms of this power to attract attention, and anxious enough to sometimes reject when they want to accept, and accept when they want to reject. It's hard being one of these boys. Older men watch them from the sidelines, drinking too much as they do. It's an attention both wanted (confirming their pulling power) and not wanted (a permanent reminder of a fate that befalls them sooner rather than later, if they don't move on).

I leave and wander up Oxford Street. Still very warm and humid. Cruised aggressively by some rough trade: two guys, together, possibly out to gay bait. No real risk given there's other people around, so I stop to talk with them for a few moments to see if I could tell. I can't, not for sure. Make an excuse, and move on.

Though I know it's probably a mistake, I want to meet up again with Ken. Still no sign. Cruise the Oxford Towers (packed) and the Midnight Shift (deserted). Wander back along Oxford Street, vaguely disconsolate. Thinking about something else I become inattentive, then aware of someone coming towards me; we are almost level before I've taken him in. I really only had time to meet his glance briefly before we passed; maybe Italian, certainly beautiful. A few seconds after we'd passed each other, we both turn. He saunters on to the next corner. I lean against a wall watching. He turns the corner out of sight. I waver, suddenly indecisive. Am I in the mood to start something new? Maybe not; leave it; maybe just walk to the corner to see if he's still there. Yes, about 40 yards down the side street, under some trees, waiting. I approach slowly and he doesn't move. He takes out his cigarettes, as I do mine. It's me who asks for the light. We exchange a few words. I invite him to walk with me. He has nowhere to take me and I can't find the $12 rooms that Ken had tried for a couple of nights back. It will have to be my place, though I'd promised Patricia and James I wouldn't take any more boys back.

He's Slovakian and his name is Marek. Although he speaks hardly any English and I know none of his languages I can tell he's apprehensive, and then realize this is because he thinks I'm taking him back to a place which I share with a 'friend' i.e. lover, and is reluctant to come, probably because he thinks I'm setting up a threesome. I try to reassure him. (Please, please don't go now, I think, but don't say.) Hesitantly he comes to the door of the flat and insists on waiting outside while I go in and plead with Patricia and James, who graciously relent. We go straight to my room.

He still seems apprehensive or maybe it's reserve. How old is he? Early twenties? I can't be sure. We have a drink but start making love before finishing even the first glass. As I enter him, I become highly sensitive to him. Out of respect certainly, but it isn't at all about holding back: right at this moment, my desire for him *is* that gentleness. I'm hopelessly in thrall to his beauty. Later everything gets more passionate, but even then it feels to me like ecstasy as homage. He remains distinct, distinctly beautiful and my pleasure right up to orgasm and far beyond is bound up with that perception.

Later we dress and go down to Oxford Street and to the Exchange. The place is packed, straight and gay, trendy and cruisy. We stand apart from the main throng, touching thighs. I want to be with him. We hold hands in a way no one else can see and I have this shocked realization that although I've done this before with partners, this is the first time I've truly wanted to. Communication is difficult but I work out he lives with some people he doesn't like. He gets tense when I try to find out more, as if afraid of something or someone. He's only recently arrived in Australia, but this is to be his home. He's clearly been lonely. We leave the Exchange and go across to the Midnight Shift. Only five others are there. We sit at the back and soon are the only ones left. Never before have I been the last to leave a gay bar – the prospect has always been too dispiriting. Not tonight. Just before we leave Marek says: 'Tonight, happy.' He says it with a smile, but also with something

else in his expression that makes me wonder again about
his situation, and the people he lives with.

We go back to Patricia and James's place, creeping in so
as not to wake them. As before, it's lovemaking through
the caress rather than the grasp, becoming sensitive to,
rather than possessing, each other. And, for me, as always,
the seeing: on this night especially the visual stays with
me – the nape of the neck, curve of the back, hardness of
the forearm, the vulnerable beauty of, well, all of him, but
especially, in this erotic recall, of the flank and abdomen.
One image especially: him half-turned away, resting on his
elbows, head and shoulders and arse arching upwards, a
poise removed from, more erotic than, either coyness or
abandon.

I discover for myself all over again that true love
doesn't have to be forever, and nor does it have to be deep
communion with another. Those are precious aspects of
love, for sure, just not the way it always has to be. As
here with Marek, I've sometimes experienced the kind of
love which isn't, initially at least, or ever, the love of deep
connection, but the superficial, beautiful connection with
the physicality of another. It's not the predatory, grossly
insensitive, desire to possess, to devour the other, and
which pornography, straight and gay, represents as the
norm in 'casual' sex. It's more like the rarifying of desire
into an attitude of erotic reverence for another, amazed
by beauty. Some writers on love warn that it's when you
give up the predatory attitude that you succumb to the
abject one and face the prospect of all the negativity in
your life condensing into an attitude of abjection before
the beautiful. I've never felt that, probably because I'm
too superficial. Disorientation and inadequacy yes, and
sometimes deep distress, but never abjection. Even if the
affair ends badly and something new hurts, some deeper
loss has been temporarily allayed, even healed.

Eventually Marek indicates that he should go, and asks
if we can meet again. I have to leave Sydney the following

day, but we arrange to meet in a week's time. It will mean
a special journey back to Sydney from Canberra but I
don't hesitate. He's adamant I must not try and get in
touch with him because of his 'friends', so I give him the
telephone number of Patricia and James's flat. He gets
up to go but I pull him back down beside me. I've never
before wanted to be with anyone as much as I do with him
now. We lie together for what must have been a couple
of hours, occasionally smoking, always sharing the same
cigarette, communicating entirely through touch. The bed
is near an open window through which, still naked, we feel
the freshness of the dawn on our skin, and later hear the
waking of others to the day, before falling asleep ourselves.

In the week I am away from Sydney, he is never out
of my thoughts. Had it been like some past encounters, I
wouldn't have been surprised to find such thoughts soon
swamped by all the trivia of daily life and eventually
washed away with them, and my deciding at the last minute
not to return after all. I can be superficial like that too.
Not this time. I think about him constantly, am painfully
restless and if anything my feelings grow in intensity. So
this time is different, although it is a difference I can't
articulate. Words fail me, or rather come to consciousness
as clichés. It seems to me now that to stand any chance
of being true to the experience of love, you need to first
renounce any aspiration to be original. So it is: in love we
struggle to articulate this intensely unique feeling only to
find ourselves uttering a platitude or cliché which tells us
it isn't unique at all, while also understanding the platitude
properly for the first time. Suddenly it resonates with
experienced meaning, even as it's useless as a means for
expressing that experience. Yet here goes: I can't wait to
see him again; I can't sleep properly for thinking about him;
first and foremost I wanted to hold him again, in my arms,
to feel the touch of his skin against mine.

I actually fly back a day early to discover he's been trying
to ring me at Patricia and James's, but hasn't left a message

or been able to make himself fully understood. I turn up at
our appointed meeting place but, as I have feared, he isn't
there. I wait for an hour, and then search all the bars for
him, without success. I keep looking, even waiting in the
exact places where we'd sat together, feeling more lonely
than if I'd never have met him. These are alienating places
for the lonely, the more so when you are missing someone
rather than looking for anyone.

I could feel something different was happening with me
in relation to him because throughout the search for him
I have zero interest in anyone else. Once I think I saw him
away in the distance in Oxford Street. My heart leaps and
then breaks (more clichés) when I discovered it isn't him
after all. Later I run into Ken; it's awkward: anything I
say will give the wrong signals so I say as little as possible,
which also gives the wrong signals. I lay awake that night
wondering about what has happened to him. When he'd
mentioned the people he lived with and insisted I couldn't
contact him because of them, he was tense. Maybe he
was in the country illegally and being exploited by those
who'd got him or were keeping him here? It's pointless
to speculate, but I can't help it. The next night I look for
him all over again and keep doing so every night until,
desolate, I have to leave Sydney. When I've left, he rings
again, but there's still no message, no address, no number.
During those last days in Australia, I develop this painfully
acute awareness of my surroundings, beautiful but so stark
and harsh, reflecting my aloneness back to me. After I've
left Australia, he rings again, several times, but Patricia or
James say that they can't make him understand, or he won't
believe, I've left the country.

I never saw him again. What would have happened had we
met again that night? I was aware even then of all the sensible
reasons for believing the affair was transient and doomed:
for a start we hardly knew each other. I was in love with his
beauty and we all know that's only skin deep. In fact, had we

met again, even a few years later, we'd both be sufficiently altered in appearance for it to be an embarrassing meeting of two who weren't exactly strangers but wished they were. Further, wasn't it just my usual thing: not love so much as a romance with love? And how could I be sure of anything after just one night together, and with the language difficulties too? And the distance barrier would have doomed it: with him in Australia and me in England, we literally could hardly have lived further apart on this earth. So, yes, it might have been that, had we met, the relationship would have proved to be nothing more than an infatuation and, because we didn't meet, I was left fixated at the point just prior to when I would have discovered it was only that.

And yet, and yet … at the time I was sure I was in love, as sure as I've ever been about anything, and I still believe that now, these years later. No, it probably wouldn't have lasted, and if it had would have been as something inconceivably different to what it was at its inception. But as it was then conceived, it would, I know, have led ineluctably to a consummation (something different from and beyond first-time intercourse or even intercourse *per se*): a precious, intensely sensual connection, an intimacy forever remembered even if, or especially because, it couldn't last and because everything afterwards was a gradual falling away, a falling back into the separation of mundane life. Unconsummated, it remained the beautiful wound: 'Beauty's wound is sharper than any weapon's and it runs through the eyes down to the soul' (Achilles Tatius, *Leucippe and Clitophon*). Beauty, skin deep, cuts to the quick.

I'm hours into the flight home, returning early on the news that a friend is terminally ill. It's dark, the flight attendants have all disappeared and some or most of the passengers are trying to sleep. I'm awake, my mind crowded with impressions of Australia, and of Marek most acutely. Then I remember too that I never got to go swimming with Lachlan. I don't want to go home.

# 8

# Reckonings

## Getting caught

When I was working at the University of Sussex, gay students would occasionally ask me to help get them out of trouble. I remember two especially. Both had been prosecuted for having sex in a public place and both were older students, having come to university later in life, rather than straight from school. They were then called mature students and they were often the most interesting people we taught. Back then they were quite common in university humanities departments; today they've all but disappeared.

Darren was around thirty, mild-mannered and rather boring socially with conversation that laboured the obvious. Like others on the gay scene, his equivalent of weather small-talk was to complain about how bad the scene was, which he'd always do, every time you met him. Sometime after graduating, and when he'd just started a teaching job, he was caught having sex in a public toilet and prosecuted. I can't now recall the exact nature of the charge against him, but, because he was being fucked at the time, it was something more serious than the usual gross indecency. I was one of several who wrote on his behalf trying to save him from being sacked from his teaching job. What I recall most clearly about Darren occurred one night about a year after this, at a mixed straight/gay disco when he tried to get off with an obviously straight, butch boy.

This disco was a weekly event organized by the Student Gaysoc, as it was then called. The straight students congregated on one side of the room, gays on the other. From the gay side, we used to take bets on which of the straight boys wanted to cross the floor but didn't yet have the courage. One of them is now a prominent member of parliament. He's out now, but as far as I can recall, although he stayed in the closet all the while he was at university he was not averse to having occasional clandestine gay sex. He was rather beautiful, so there was plenty of willing partners, including a boyfriend of mine at the time.

The guy Darren was interested in was quite different – rather stridently straight and seemingly dull-witted too, because he didn't seem to realize which side of the room he was on or that Darren was coming on to him. It wasn't bravado on Darren's part – the cruise was furtive and initially no one else apart from me realized what was going on, and Darren didn't know I was watching. They were sitting together on a table and Darren was rubbing his thigh against the man's, the more persistently the more he failed to notice. When eventually he did realize what was happening the guy was hysterically outraged and for a while I thought he was going to attack Darren and I moved to intervene. The expression on Darren's face was unforgettable: abject torment. This wasn't fear of being assaulted or even of an embarrassing scene. I saw it in a flash – for him cruising was a terrible compulsion; he just couldn't help himself. I've never forgotten that expression: desire as compulsion and torment – something our demand for gay liberation couldn't fully acknowledge because to do so might give credence to those who wanted to pathologize gay desire. We wanted to say that the torment was down to the distortions of oppression, and in part it obviously was, but there was more to be said about the darker side of desire and it was the task of liberation to say that too. Mostly it didn't. Within a couple of years of that encounter, Darren was dead from HIV/AIDS.

I've always seen gay subculture as embodying truths larger than itself. This isn't because I think it needs vindication or special pleading in such terms; rather it's because I found starkly revealed there things which were true also more generally of mainstream culture, though only mutedly, or less extremely, less obviously so. In the context of HIV/AIDS, sexual compulsion made those like Darren utterly vulnerable. In mainstream culture, too, we witness the vulnerabilities and the damage of sexual compulsion, but here masked and mitigated more effectively by power, money, status and convention.

Darren was an ordinary kind of guy. When I think back to those on the scene who were, by contrast, the most outrageous, interesting, distinctive, they were if anything even more vulnerable. That's partly because in subcultures there are fewer safety nets, also because some of those drawn to subcultures enjoy the risk. Some were memorable because in their case the cliché was apposite: the brighter they shone the quicker they burned out; the most fabulous being also the most fragile. Most significantly, there were those whose creativity thrived on risk, danger and vulnerability. Not that they were necessarily artists; some were or aspired to be, while others, like Oscar Wilde, put their genius into their lives, or intended to, but, unlike him, didn't bother devoting their talent to art. At the time, life on the scene seemed enough, but if they survived the danger, the risk and the burn out, it rarely seemed so with hindsight. With some of them I couldn't be sure because I never knew where they ended up; they just disappeared, and were barely missed in a scene obsessed with the new, the fashionable and the young.

The other student I helped was Graham. He'd also been caught having sex in a public place somewhere in Manchester and was also prosecuted. He insisted on pleading not guilty, although everyone told him he was wasting his time, and with good reason: not only had the police observed him having sex with another man, but that very man had been prosecuted a short time previously, and pleaded guilty. Moreover – and this was the prosecution's killerhand – that same man was their main witness against Graham. He just couldn't win,

yet still he insisted on that not guilty plea. He asked me to
go up to Manchester to be a character witness. I agreed, and
the night before the court case Graham and some other gay
friends gave me a makeover. The idea was to transform me
into a staid-looking, married academic, as reliable and boring
as they come. My leather jacket was replaced with a tweed
one, jeans with pressed trousers, sneakers with brogues, a
wedding ring placed on the correct finger, hair neatly parted
and brushed/greased down. I enjoyed playing the part. I think
it was my first time in drag, but by no means my last. I stayed
over in Manchester for several days and it never stopped
raining.

On the day of the trial, even Graham's barrister tried
to get him to change his plea to guilty, telling him his case
was hopeless, but still he refused. His reasons seemed to
me a strange mix of paranoid stubbornness and gay activist
courage. The main prosecution witness, the man Graham had
been having sex with, appeared completely broken. He was
black, from the Caribbean, if we read his accent correctly. It
was obvious he'd been closeted and his own prosecution had
wrecked him – and his marriage. I decided Graham was right
to plead not guilty.

Apart from me, we had another witness – a young American
woman who very much liked the company of gay men and
whom Graham had befriended a year or so earlier and then
married. It was a familiar story: she had visa problems and
was going to have to leave the country and by becoming
Graham's wife she was able to stay. It was truly a marriage of
convenience, not uncommon between gay men and women in
need of a passport or visa. Graham wasn't remotely straight
and she probably wouldn't have been his friend if he had been.
She repaid the favour magnificently. There she was, the young
newly wed, deeply distressed yet determined to defend her
husband, tearfully gripping the dock in front of her so that yet
another recently acquired wedding ring was on full display for
the jury to see. On one occasion, she turned to address the jury
directly, and with passionate conviction declared: 'I know my

husband and I know he would never do such a terrible thing as this.' It was pure theatre and I was lost in admiration.

Incredibly, the jury, none of whom were young, returned a verdict of not guilty. I can't imagine that the jurors actually believed he hadn't done it. After all, there was no reason why the main witness, the person with whom he'd been having sex, and who had already pleaded guilty, should have been lying, and none was even suggested by the defence. Perhaps it was simply the case that the jury believed that as a newlywed, he shouldn't be punished for what he'd one. I'd also like to think, but doubt, that they were as incensed as we were at the sight of that broken prosecution witness. The judge was visibly annoyed and refused the defence costs. Outside we passed one of the juror's smoking a cigarette. Whether the grin he gave us was knowing or not, I can't say, but he wished Graham good luck.

We were euphoric, and that night was a wild one: Graham picked up a gay policeman and I had some quick sex in a toilet with someone I later learned was an MEP. I guess you could say we were incorrigible. So euphoric were we that we might even have had sex with each other, except that it was from Graham I'd learned how certain relationships between gay men and women and, even more so, between gay men, could be the closer for being non-sexual. In the former case, sex just isn't an issue, whereas in the latter, there is an unspoken understanding that this is a friendship in which sex is prohibited, and which might be destroyed were that prohibition transgressed. The friendship between me and Graham was like that.

On the same night, after Graham and I became separated, I cruised another guy in a club; his name was Keith, he was twenty-one and though he wouldn't come back with me then we met the next day and spent some time together. He lived in one of those large Victorian houses that are split into rented flats and finally take on that drabness which was always their destiny and which their architecture always seemed to promise. His was a small flat which he shared with a straight woman lodger. It was a dismal place – low-wattage light bulbs with yellowed, probably nicotine stained shades, damp walls with flaking plaster, no blinds or curtains. His bedroom was empty apart from the bed, a wardrobe, and a large floppy Pierrot doll sitting slumped on the mantelpiece, a present from his lodger. As we made love, it watched us with its sad eyes and big black falling tear. I came rather noisily and Keith started hushing me up in case the lodger heard.

'She mustn't know I'm gay', he whispered urgently.

'Yeah, well,' I said after regaining my composure, 'that might be something of a lost cause', knowing full well from the briefest of eye contact with her earlier not only that she knew, but that she wanted me to know she knew.

'No, the thing is', whispered Keith, 'her Mum knows my Mum and she doesn't know I'm gay.'

I started to rehearse in my mind a gentle lecture about the importance of coming out to family, friends and lodgers, but kept getting drawn back to the Pierrot, so still and sad and silent, as the rain pattered persistently at the window, while dawn light slowly displaced the weak glare of the single bulb, and I remained silent too. And besides, Keith had fallen asleep. I returned home to Brighton, and Keith and I spoke on the phone a few times and then he suddenly disappeared. About a year later, he rang me late one night from San Francisco, very excited about the scene there and high on something. That was the last contact we had. I hope he's still alive.

Graham went to live in London where we had a few more nights out together. Memories of that period are blurred, not least because we mixed alcohol, dope and poppers freely, the effects of which were in my case pleasantly compounded by the heavy duty anti-depressants I was on. I recall clearly the last time we met. We'd been to Heaven (the club) and somewhere along the way fell in with someone called Joker, that being the name he both answered, and lived up to, as I was to discover. We all three went by taxi to a sparsely wooded parkland area which Graham knew to have recently become a lively cruising ground. We'd been smoking some of

Joker's joints, which packed a vicious hit because they were also soaked in amyl – a combination at once dizzying, slightly sickening yet irresistible, or at least bringing you back for more – and drinking neat gin from a half bottle. Quite soon after we arrived Graham went off with someone, and as he disappeared into the darkness, he laughed in a way I couldn't quite identify and have never forgotten. Shortly after that I fell over, and lay there looking up at the sky trying unsuccessfully to remember some lines of Yeats about the moonlit night. I fancied I could see the galaxies revolving, but since this was with my eyes open or shut, I eventually conceded it must be the narcotics. Someone approached and I realized, as he got up very close, mainly from his stagger, that it was Joker. He lay down beside me, one hand fumbling for my groin, declaring: 'I love you, I always have.'

'Joker you tosser', I replied. 'It's me. We came here together. Remember?'

His blank and empty 'Oh' was followed by a very long pause, during which I imagined I could now trace in the slowly revolving night sky the not so slow obliteration of his and my brain cells. This with my eyes open, but not shut. Then he said, 'Well, that might work too.' Another long pause before he added, 'The thing is I'm too wasted to do anything standing up, and you're the only person lying down.'

'Well', I replied, 'I'm too wasted to even think of doing anything. Period. Give me a drink'.

So we lay there for a while trying to drink neat gin but with difficulty. Then Joker staggered off.

I must have passed out or fallen asleep because suddenly I felt a mild stab of pain in my side and someone uttering a hushed, shocked, curse. Then another voice: 'Fuck, a body!' and the first one again: 'Fuck!'

Why is it that, when surprised, people are never original in their expletives? Although it wasn't yet apparent to me, there were two men, one of whom had stumbled into me – understandable so, given that, in cruising grounds you tend not to pay much attention to anything below groin height. Their first thought (I later realized) was that I was injured, possibly even dead, as a result of queer-bashing.

I struggled to speak, and managed to eventually: 'No, it's OK, I'm er, uh just ... just ...'. I hadn't any idea how, or the inner resources, to finish this sentence. They misconstrued my vacancy as embarrassment, and one of them stifled a relieved giggle.

Me: 'Oh. No. I er, uh ...'. Another sentence I couldn't finish. So they moved off with a parting: 'Have a nice ... [long pause, more giggling] ... night.'

I examined the night sky some more, trying again to recall the Yeats but only getting fragments ... moonlight, something about complexity ...

The ravenous hunger dope induces eventually got me to my feet. I didn't have a clue as to which part of London I was in, and, come to think of it, still don't. I walked a while before finding a taxi, got back to Graham's place, ate what was left in the fridge, and slept for a few hours before heading for Victoria, via Soho. Graham still wasn't back by the time I left. I was horny in the most tedious and hungover of ways and had sex with a man in the toilet of a Soho porn cinema. Hungrily sucking me off, he kept pausing and looking up, as if he'd just remembered, or perhaps just forgotten, something important, or failed to hear something I'd said, and each time he did so he would ask if I was into water sports. God knows what he was on. Or maybe it was early onset dementia.

Then on to Victoria and the train back to Brighton. Sitting there trying to sleep, they at last came to me correctly, the Yeats's lines:

A starlit or a moonlit dome disdains
All that man is;
All mere complexities,
The fury and the mire of human veins.

When he wrote that, I doubt Yeats had water sports in mind, but who knows? And anyway, that apart, it seemed apposite.

The mere (brilliant word) complexities, the fury and the mire of human veins, acted out against the backdrop of a sublimely indifferent universe. Then a flashback to a class: a student expostulating angrily that he couldn't take seriously a poet (Yeats) who didn't have sex until he was thirty-one. As if fucking were a necessary condition of being a good poet, and virginity a sufficient condition of being a bad one. Was this the endpoint of liberation? At the time I didn't know what to say, but in that railway carriage it suddenly struck me as obvious that teaching is a hugely overrated activity, and that you should only ever have to teach people you love, or at least like, or at the very least, respect. This was the first time I'd felt this with such intensity; thereafter I felt it frequently.

I gazed at the countryside, its cleanness and openness seeming like a more mundane kind of disdain than Yeats's night sky, yet still reason enough to turn back to the unclean, crowded cover of the city, and the sense of anticipation which that first rush of warm stale air in the underground always bought – along with thoughts of suicide, though not, in this instance, of my own. It was the smell and feel of that underground air which was my most vivid impression of London when I first visited the city on my own as a fifteen year old, and this was probably because, just before, I'd read something in my father's newspaper about the frequency of suicides on the underground. I can't recall the exact numbers back then, only that I was disturbed and fascinated by their regularity. I still am: warm stale wind, dust in the eyes; the underground wind of a city, an old wind and an old city, with its intimations of pleasures shot through with loneliness. The sensations were excitingly new, yet stained with the loneliness of the millions who'd gone before.

I would often experience this temptation to return to the city just as I was leaving it. Sometimes I actually did, getting off at the next station, crossing the tracks and boarding the first train back. Not this time: I needed to work out how I was going to wing the next day's classes which I already knew I wasn't going to prepare for. Depressed and bored, I went and jerked off in the train toilet.

Although that night when he disappeared, laughing, was the last time I saw Graham, we did speak again a few years later. He phoned to say he was in more trouble with the police, this time for theft, and would I be a character witness again. I can't now recall why, but I refused. Although at the time he didn't seem to mind much, after that we lost touch completely until, years later, his name came up at a party and someone remarked that they had just heard he'd recently committed suicide. This person had no idea why Graham had killed himself, but several others present, who remembered him, or claimed to, speculated self-importantly on the reasons why, before the conversation drifted on to a recent production at Glyndebourne, which also featured a suicide, and how gloriously it had been done.

Over the years my memory of Graham has revolved around the way he laughed as he went off into the darkness that night; vividly recalled despite, or because of, being unseeable: a sudden, spontaneous, unexpected, inexplicable, expression of delight. Fleeting, too, and unusual to hear: cruising in places like that was typically governed by a ritualistic rule of silence, like being in a library or a church. Unusual for another reason too: I was familiar with gay men on the scene who laughed cynically, mockingly, ironically, with forced hilarity or camp exaggeration, but rarely with the spontaneous delight I heard then. I've often wondered since what prompted it. Obviously I'll never know now. But the thing is, even if Graham were still alive and I were able to ask him, I know he wouldn't remember.

# The test

Identity wise, I'm locked into gay culture. Everyone I know assumes I'm exclusively gay and I'm going along with that. It's obvious that some close relationships I have with women simply aren't open to becoming erotic, even if they or I want that possibility, because of those assumptions.

That seems wrong, even though being thought of as exclusively gay makes my relationships with women easier, more honest, and sometimes closer than they were when I'd been perceived as exclusively straight. But it seems deceitful to pretend to be something I'm not. Anyway, my troublesome feelings of boredom, restlessness and curiosity are now chaffing against the confines of gay culture: like any other culture, there are pressures to conform, pressures which I react against. Before I could entertain any kind of sexual relationship with a woman though, I need to take the HIV test.

Actually I should have taken it long before, and I cannot now offer any justification for not having done so, or why I felt those women were entitled to a consideration I hadn't always shown to gay partners, although I had never lied about my status in a gay context. If anyone wanted to know I said I honestly didn't know but added, only sometimes, that I feared the worst.

There was a charity in The Steine in Brighton that offered free HIV-testing and I went there. It was underfunded and overworked. I had a preliminary assessment in which I had to give a candid account of my sexual history and behaviours, and on the basis of that was advised I needed not just an HIV test but a raft of others, too, and that this would take longer – from memory around ten (working) days instead of the usual six. I was to ring them in about two weeks time. The wait was tough but I threw myself into some practical work, restoring an old car. It was work which narrowed the mind, drew it out from itself, focusing it on the task in hand and offering the escape of mindless concentration.

After the ten (working) days are up, I phone the clinic and am told that yes, my tests are back, but can't be given over the phone: I have to come in and receive them personally. So this was it: truth time. A friend who has recently been diagnosed as HIV-positive says something which makes an impression on me. I'd asked him if he felt angry or bitter at the way things had turned out for him. He says he didn't, adding matter of factly: 'Sooner or later we always pay the price.' I know him well enough to know he isn't being moralistic or even fatalistic, just realistic. He isn't going to rage at fate, or the government for not funding AIDS awareness; nor is he going to complain bitterly of his bad luck, or blame anyone partner, although he does confess to the occasional futile speculation as to which one had been the one. He didn't want to beat up on himself either. He is, he says, just trying to take responsibility. With his example I feel ready, or at least hope I am, to also take responsibility for bad news.

In those days, for the majority, a positive result still meant a death sentence, and an unpleasant one at that. I remember thinking it important that I dress appropriately for such a momentous occasion, but had no idea what that should be. The choice of reading matter while waiting was much easier: a collection of the poems of Fulke Greville, put together by Thom Gunn. It was a long wait – like I said, they were underfunded and overworked. Despite or because of anxiety I was able to concentrate on the verse, and began to understand Gunn's interest in Greville.

Eventually I'm called in. The clinician is clearly uncomfortable. So it's positive, I think. OK, so I'm paying the price; I'm ready: take responsibility. And then he speaks: 'I'm sorry Jonathan, there's been a mistake in the paperwork and your results aren't back after all.'

The long wait has been because they were trying to find the paperwork ... underfunded and overworked ... come back in another four days ... I'd felt prepared for the bad news of a positive result; whether I would have been in the event I don't know, but am definitely not prepared for this.

I left the clinic around 11.30 in the morning and although midsummer, it's a grey day with drizzling rain and a cold blustering offshore wind. I walk aimlessly along the Brighton seafront in the direction of Kemp Town. The sea is quite rough and I find myself wondering, not for the first time, how easy it is to drown. I'm not suicidal, just thinking about a point in the future when illness might make it the preferred option. Also, I'm genuinely uncertain, having read somewhere that it was a painful way to die, elsewhere that it was peaceful, at least at the very end.

The clouds grow greyer and descend lower, and the drizzle turns into a steady rain, falling into and merging with the sea so effortlessly and seductively after the momentary disruption of first impact. Before long I'm soaked. Then I realize I'm in an area where Rachel, a colleague and friend, lives. I find her house, knock on her door and she is welcoming and supportive when I tell her what had happened, although for reasons not clear to me at the time, I play it down. I stay a couple of hours and we talk easily about many things other than HIV.

The next few days were difficult. My resolve unravelled and I became sure I was going to pay the price. I had a bit of a cough and felt convinced this was an early symptom. Knowing how miserable an AIDS death could be, I was resolved not to linger to the end. I knew a sympathetic doctor – maybe she could get me a large enough dose of morphine so I could end things on my terms. After that early experience of it in hospital after the road accident, I'd become a believer in morphine and couldn't think of better way to go. Strangely though, its later effects on me have been different. Morphine bliss now induces not a sense of possibility and potential but a feeling of perfect peace, an inner weightlessness, a calm wanting for nothing. In this, it strikes me as the perfect 'Western' narcotic, giving instant access (short-lived and at a price) to a state of mind which in Eastern philosophies requires years of physical renunciation and psychic discipline.

No – I could never ask this this doctor to take the risk. It would have to be (again) the hose pipe through the window

of the car in the garage. Would it be that easy? I knew that
the knowledge they are going to die engenders in some people
with terminal illnesses a fierce desire to live on to the very end,
to cling to whatever is left of life at any cost. And what about
my parents? They lived on the other side of the world, in New
Zealand. Could I get away with not telling them? Well, that
wouldn't exactly be taking responsibility. I also found myself
thinking about who I really cared about in the event of facing
an early death and the answer was surprising, even slightly
shocking. I realized that there were certain people I loved more
than I consciously acknowledged, and others who perhaps I
didn't love as much as I had thought. Death, the great leveller?
I suppose so, insofar as it obliterates distinction of wealth and
status. Yet here was the prospect of death compelling me to
discriminate, to put aside sentiment, convention and habit. I
never did fully act upon what I'd discovered about my feelings
across those three bad days, and I regret that. It seems now
like a form of cowardice.

By the time I return to the clinic, I've talked myself into
expecting the worst. This time I see a different person and
he looks almost cheerful, something I interpret as a brave
face for my benefit. Just as I sit down his telephone goes.
Oh Christ. Thankfully he quickly gets rid of the caller, but
in the 20 seconds or so it takes him to do so, and with the
hyper-awareness that anxiety induces (strange the way you
either become aware of everything or nothing), I notice
there are two half-drunk cups of tea or coffee on his desk,
and a lot of paperwork in disarray; that he is thin to the
point of emaciation, and on the wall is a large safe-sex
poster which just now has a poignant, lonely immediacy –
for me. He put the phone down and speaks: 'Sorry about
that Jonathan. I'm happy to say that you seem to be in the
clear. The HIV-test shows negative and we found no sign
of any other STD.'

I can't recall much of what follows after that except
that he gently admonishes me for my past behaviours

and asks me to practice safe sex, henceforth. I want to ask him about his own status but don't because I fear it would seem presumptuous, and anyway his professional etiquette probably forbids such conversations. Outside I feel disbelief, exhilaration and notice for the first time that it's a beautiful morning, with a fresh breeze, scudding clouds casting fast-moving shadows, the sun glinting on the sea. The seagulls are flocking and wheeling, and, as always, but only now fully realized, the cacophony of their calls sounds clearer and louder in the morning air than later in the day. This changes everything; suddenly the future is once more full of possibility. I go into a pub on the seafront to celebrate, and after a first drink call some friends from a payphone with the good news. Rachel is the first, and with her I keep the details brief and to the point, but to a gay friend who I've recently been teasingly trying to seduce, I relate all the things I could remember I've been tested for, including HIV, report that I'm deliciously clean on all counts, and that, as a consequence; 'I have just been officially and medically certified as, right this minute, the safest fuck in all of Brighton. I intend to remain so for one hour, and am offering you first refusal.'

A little forward perhaps, but then there are those who find the sassy approach disarming.

'Well J,' he replies, 'I'm pleased for you, though it doesn't change the fact that you're a dirty little player who takes it up against the wall.'

'So that's a yes then?'

'No, it's a no then.'

'As in "no means yes"?'

'No. "No" as in, "go fuck yourself".'

And so our flirtatious banter trips gaily on, one endearment fast on the heels of the next. But I'm touched and chastened by his parting words: 'Seriously J, one of the things this means is that you haven't infected anyone else. Now it's up to you whether you keep it that way.'

He was right, of course, and I returned to the bar to get quietly wasted on my own. And although I can't claim that it was there and then that I determined to do so, it is true that from then on I mostly either practiced safe sex or abstained from having it. But perhaps the strangest outcome of this episode, utterly unexpected by me at the time, is that a couple of weeks later, Rachel and I began a fifteen-year relationship and had two children together, both daughters.

# 9

# Oblivion and touch, 1993

This day dawns fresh and bright after the previous night's storm: clear clean air, glistening rain-washed hills, cloudless brilliant blue sky. A perfect new day, perfect, in part, because sublimely oblivious of its own past.

As sentient beings, we're attracted to inanimate nature, yet ambivalently so because it has something we lack, or rather lacks something we have. We see the blindness behind the beauty, the silence inside the movement; it attracts us, but in a way which tells us we're alone:

> In spring ... Violets came and daffodils. But the stillness and the brightness of the day were as strange as the chaos and tumult of night, with the trees standing there, and the flowers standing there, looking before them, looking up, yet beholding nothing, eyeless, and so terrible. (Virginia Woolf, *To the Lighthouse*)

Memory and desire exile us from the sublime purity of inanimate nature, making us hostages of both a past and a future. We grieve in relation to the past, and desire in relation to the future, while the fleeting present is where desire and grieving merge. No wonder then if we yearn for the peace that passeth all understanding, although, for the irreligious, oblivion is probably the closest we're going to get.

I'm looking out on this perfect day from a place I used to ride out to with a friend. Tim was a beautiful blend of gentleness and self-confidence, someone who was completely at ease not only with being gay, which he'd known he was from a very early age, but also with the fact that he loved to be fucked – something else he'd known from an early age. We slept together only once and that didn't really work out because we confirmed in bed what we probably already knew out of it, which was that we weren't much attracted to each other sexually. It didn't matter, and we became friends and would sometimes ride out of Brighton on my bike to this spot. We would park up the bike, chain our helmets to it, and go walking. Although our friendship was casual I realized I loved him in a light-hearted way because whatever he said or did held my interest and attention, was endearing. At this time, I had to pretend professionally to be interested in people who actually bored me, colleagues just as much as students. Tim never did; I was always happy, softly elated, at being with him not least because we each seemed to intuit what the other was thinking and feeling.

We cruised together occasionally, but the time with him I remember most clearly was the last time, and it was typically inconsequential – a midsummer's night in Brighton when, unusually, we left the Curtain Club early and, on impulse, went across the road down to the beach. The air was completely still and there were no waves or surf; the sea barely lapped at the shore. We lay on the steeply sloped part of the beach, moulding the stones to our bodies and Tim rolled a joint. We didn't talk much, but he told me he'd at last finished his thesis (he was a graduate student in the sciences), that he'd got no specific plans yet, and trying to decide on the future was daunting but he hoped to be able to travel and work abroad, perhaps South America, before settling anywhere. I hadn't realized until that moment how sorry I'd be to see him go but didn't say so because he did need to go. So we stayed there for a while, smoking the joint, watching sheet lightning over or across the channel, the storm a long way off, occasional thunder distant and receding.

The last time I saw Tim, he was on the door of the university Gaysoc disco taking the entrance money. As he gave me my change, he gently squeezed my hand and gave me the lightest and most tender of passing kisses, telling me he was heading for London. We couldn't talk because there was a queue, but agreed we would get together before he went. I truly meant to and think he did as well, but we didn't, and not long after that I went abroad while he went to London and we lost touch. I heard of his death a few years later, not even having known he'd been ill. He was one of the first to die, and he died quickly, compared with some of those who died later. I know it must have been a painful, humiliating and lonely death.

Lifting out of a depression, I've returned to this place where Tim and I used to come. I'm still feeling vulnerable, with undertows of longing, now drawing me back, now forward, along with a melancholy wonder at being alive at all. Looking across this landscape on such a beautiful day, so fresh and bright, it's not death I feel vulnerable to but life, in all its sheer, terrible contingency: I'm here while Tim is not, but it could easily have been the other way round, and yet nothing about this day, or this place, would have been different if it had. Truly then a sublime landscape.

Remembering the past can be a hopeless act of love, but an act of love nevertheless. The crash helmet I gave Tim to wear was slightly too large, and, because he wasn't used to riding pillion he'd hold on tightly to me with both hands, meaning he could never spare a hand to adjust the helmet, so that when he got off the bike it might be slightly lopsided. I see him now, standing there, arms by his side, grinning, with the helmet askew, head tilted back and to one side, so he could see me.

And I can still feel him behind me on the bike, his arms around me, body up as close to mine as he could get, the inside of his thighs pressing against the outside of mine, vulnerable yet trusting. We tell so much about another from the way they touch us. I remember another friend telling me that she knew her lover had been unfaithful to her the instant he touched her afterwards. Sometimes, if Tim became apprehensive, he would hold on to me the more tightly. I felt it acutely, and would slow down, while never knowing for sure if he was even aware of doing so.

So yes, I came to love Tim, and whether that was despite, or because, of the sex between us not working, I can't say and don't really care. What I do know though it that the love was no less homoerotic for becoming chaste, and that his touch was no less sensual for having being released from desire. I realize now, the touch of people like him have always done more than drugs or therapy in pulling me back from the seductions of oblivion. For now, I choose touch, or the memory of touch, over oblivion.

I also returned to the church where I'd seen the child's grave and the footprint in the cement.

It's good to see the missing pane in the stain glass window has been replaced. As always the depiction of Christ on the cross draws and holds my gaze, and, again as always, I search in vain for even a hint of the promise of redemption it's supposed to embody. Even so, I regard it with humility, because what that image of a mutilated, suffering being does tell me, an unbeliever, is that the mysteries of desire and consciousness began with a fall from the purity of inanimate being.

I feel a little wiser in desire and lonelier as a consequence. I realize, too, that I have thought about some things for too long, and so no longer understand them; thinking now is different, feeling less a quest for understanding than a heightened awareness. Which means it matters less when it's inconclusive, which is often. One of the myths of human thinking, allowing us to create as well as destroy, is that we must penetrate down to the core inner truth (essence) and out to the absolute truth (universal). For me, now, to think deeply is to arrive in this hinterland of indeterminacy where meaning thins out, like a beam of light projected into the night sky, illuminating nothing, and calling attention only to itself before eventually dissipating.

I also have this realization that to make the journey back from depression to life, I need to have the courage of my own unimportance. In youth, the realization of one's insignificance is wounding; later, it's merely regrettable; later still, it's almost consoling. Even so, the narcissistic wound only ever finally heals in death. But past failures, past hurts, even against the mother, against lovers, now seem fragilely redeemable in the present if I can embrace my own unimportance.

Being alive is getting slightly easier. Elation becomes possible again although it's a vulnerable elation, very different from both the manic elation of bipolar conditions, and of the drug-induced high; different from the first (bipolar) because not so desperately driven, and from the second (drugs) because the sense of possibility is less inwardly fantasized, more outwardly aware. It's an elation inseparable from being, from being alive, but lacking the 'density' of pleasure or gratification; it's so much thinner than that – ethereal almost, having a translucence through which the other of pleasure filters through. The pleasurable lightness of being perhaps, and reminiscent of that slow-burn elation I've often gone in search of, although being this close to depression, albeit on the way out rather than in, I'd say rather that it's a trembling or shimmering elation, like a shaft of light in water.

Water as metaphor, and so much more than that, because I also associate this fragile elation with the regenerative influence of rain, as when Van Morrison writes of walking in gardens all wet with rain, and never growing so old again, or George Herbert's lines from more than three centuries earlier:

> Grief melts away
> Like snow in May,
> As if there were no such cold thing.
> ...
> After so many deaths I live and write;
> I once more smell the dew and rain.

The idea that the young flirt with death because they think themselves immortal is less than half true; it's also because in them the narcissistic wound is still raw. I now think my own self-inflicted encounters with death had a lot to do with that wound, which is another way of saying I grew up slowly, if at all. Yet the immaturity of youth sometimes achieves an intensity of being which, for all its recklessness, is on the side of life. If we survive it we may or may not be glad of having done so, and what we feel about this probably depends on how much failure we've embraced in adulthood, of how much failure we've mistaken for success, and how acutely we realize that survival is not a good in itself. We can die just by staying alive, living becoming a dying to life. Which means that if we do survive, we incur an even greater obligation to life as against survival: not just to stay alive but to stay alive to life itself.

Romantics believe the transience of something can enhance rather than debilitate its beauty, albeit in a sad kind of way: 'Life is the rose's hope while yet unblown' (Keats). It works well with roses and even people so long as we don't love them. I can't accept that love, except maybe romantic love at its most narcissistic, can ever be reconciled to the loss of the loved, and it wouldn't be love if it could.

Wittgenstein famously says: 'Death is not an event in life: we do not live to experience death.' That's a philosophical rationalization, a rationalized truth. He also says: 'If we take eternity to mean not infinite temporal duration but timelessness, then eternal life belongs to those who live in the present.' That's also cleverly said, but I think it's impossible for sentient beings like us to live entirely in the present. The passing of time, which makes it so urgent to seize the day, is also what prevents us from doing so; because through time, in time, the day slips through our hands. So perhaps the most meaningful way of living in the present may be retrospectively, from a point in the future; to imaginatively project ourselves into a future and look back at the here and now as already gone; to seek to live the present from a future in which it is already past. From this future remove from it, we may have a slightly better chance of appreciating the present before it's gone. That in turn might help us live more intimately because there's a poignant kind of forgiveness deriving from a heightened awareness of loss and realizing something is gone forever alleviates at least some of the hurt that went with it. People who can't forgive are locked into a past kept always present. Conversely, we may forgive just because we experience loss, and mistake forgiveness for love. There are worse mistakes to make.

Tim and the others: their being alive moved life itself into the sun, irrespective of whether they were my lover or not; I might have wished they were, but I didn't need that to be so to feel this soft elation in their presence, in their being, their being here. Their just being alive lifted the tedium of life, made it worth being alive. Their not being here is a wounding absence experienced most acutely as a loss of touch, as much the passing touch of the everyday, as the embrace of the night, or rather the dawn:

> He got up to go but I pulled him back down beside me. I've never since wanted to be with anyone as much as I did with him then. We lay together for what must have been a couple of hours, occasionally smoking, always sharing the same cigarette, communicating entirely through touch. The bed was near an open window through which, still naked, we felt the freshness of the dawn on our skin, and later heard the waking of others to the day, before falling asleep ourselves.

CPSIA information can be obtained
at www.ICGtesting.com
Printed in the USA
LVOW10s0214130218
566382LV00013B/289/P